GLOBAL PUBLIC
MANAGEMENT

GLOBAL PUBLIC MANAGEMENT
Cases and Comments

EDITORS

KATHE CALLAHAN
Rutgers University

DOROTHY OLSHFSKI
Rutgers University

ERWIN SCHWELLA
University of Stellenbosch

SAGE Publications
Thousand Oaks ▪ London ▪ New Delhi

For information:

Sage Publications, Inc.
2455 Teller Road
Thousand Oaks, California 91320
E-mail: order@sagepub.com

Sage Publications Ltd.
1 Oliver's Yard
55 City Road
London EC1Y 1SP
United Kingdom

Sage Publications India Pvt. Ltd.
B-42, Panchsheel Enclave
Post Box 4109
New Delhi 110 017 India

Library of Congress Cataloging-in-Publication Data

Global public management: cases and comments/[edited by] Kathe Callahan, Dorothy Olshfski, Erwin Schwella.
    p. cm.
Includes index.
ISBN 0-7619-2796-4 (pbk.)
    1. Public administration—Case studies. I. Callahan, Kathe. II. Olshfski, Dorothy F. III. Schwella, Erwin.
JF1351.G567 2005
351—dc22

                                            2004014079

Printed on acid-free paper in the United States of America.

05   06   07   08   09   10   9   8   7   6   5   4   3   2   1

Acquisitions Editor:	Al Bruckner
Editorial Assistant:	MaryAnn Vail
Production Editor:	Tracy Alpern
Copy Editor:	Ruth Saavedra
Typesetter:	C&M Digitals (P) Ltd.
Indexer:	Sheila Bodell
Cover Designer:	Edgar Abarca

Contents

Introduction   ix

CASES   1

1. Parking Tickets and School Bonds   3
   Suzanne J. Piotrowski

2. The Education of the Police Commissioner   6
   Erwin Schwella

3. Community Outreach Chaos   13
   Kathryn Hammond

4. Performance Reports   17
   Karel van der Molen and Belinda Van Wyk

5. The Price of Rebuilding a War-Torn Town   20
   Bojana Blagojevic

6. University Games   24
   Helen Paxton

7. Redevelopment and the Community   27
   Mark Swilling

8. Reporting the Local News   33
   Terence J. Reidy

9. Returning Home to Serve   38
   Frederic Bogui

10. Computer Problems at the Library   41
    Ray Schwartz

11. Getting Support for Good Works   43
    Janna Ataiants

12. An Office Romance   48
    RaJade Berry

13. Moving Up in the Organization   52
    Belinda Van Wyk

14. Training Grant Decisions   54
    Richard Blake and Paulette Laubsch

15. Getting the Staff On Board   57
    Kamal Chavda

16. Starting the New Job   60
    Jessica de Koninck

17. Friendships and the Job   64
    Myung Jean Chun

18. The Workplace of Doom   67
    Willa Bruce

COMMENTS   71

Case 1   73
    Mel Dubnick, Yilin Hou, and Babette Smit

Case 2   79
    Richard C. Kearney, Rosanne Manghisi,
    and Nancy Soper DuBro

Case 3   85
    Cheryl Simrell King, Lyle Wray, and Kaifeng Yang

Case 4   91
    Maria P. Aristigueta, Andrew Bednarek,
    and Harry J. Hayes

Case 5   96
    Eve Annecke, Phil Morgan, and Lyuba Palyvoda

Case 6   102
    Jacques Bojin, Fanie Cloete, and Susan Morley

Case 7   108
    Jennifer Brinkerhoff and Derick Brinkerhoff,
    Vache Gabrielian, and Adriaan Schout

Case 8   116
    Steve Adubato, I. H. Meyer, and Susan C. Paddock

Case 9   122
    Valiant Clapper, Robert Cunningham,
    and Andi Zhamierashvili

Case 10   128
    Jonathan Justice, Gail Kenny,
    and Sarmistha Rina Majumdar

Case 11   133
     Koen M. Becking, Peter F. Haruna,
     and Jyl Josephson

Case 12   139
     Alma Joseph, Changhwan Mo,
     and Meredith Newman

Case 13   144
     Janet Foley Orosz, Yusuf Sayed, and Naomi Wish

Case 14   150
     Hedy Isaacs, Willy McCourt, and Ethel Williams

Case 15   157
     Tao Hoe Eom, Ray Gonzales, and Ton van der Wiel

Case 16   163
     Domonic A. Bearfield, Jon Foster Pedley,
     and Navdeep Mathur

Case 17   170
     Seok-Hwan Lee, Carl W. Nelson,
     and Francine Widrich

Case 18   177
     Raphael J. Caprio, Annie Hondeghem,
     and Andrea Quarantillo

Index   187

About the Editors   193

Introduction

Managerial Education

There is only one way to learn how to be a manager: experience. If you examine research and study textbooks, you will get some good ideas about how to do things differently and how to think about what you have already done; and all of this will help you *think about* how to be a good manager. Thinking like a good manager is very important. However, it is experience that helps you *act* like a good manager. Managing people and situations in the workplace is a behavior-based activity, and behaving is different from thinking. This is the difference between knowing what to do and knowing how to do it.

Experience helps us know how to manage. But not all experience has to be first-hand, personal experience. Vicarious experience is the practice in managing that we get from viewing others' experience and thinking about it like it was our own. Vicarious experience comes in the form of watching behaviors and then thinking about them in management terms. Watching takes a number of forms: You can actually watch someone deal with a situation, or you can view experiences through biography, fiction, movies, or case studies.

Actual experience is truly a potent teacher. All of us, at one time or another, have heard someone say after a particularly bad interaction with someone in the office, "I'll never do that again." Or alternatively, after being involved in an activity that really worked, "I have got to remember to do that next time." Experience teaches.

Vicarious experience also can be a powerful teacher, if you view observation as learning. Watch a really good manager conduct a meeting: What is it that that manager actually did to lead you to believe that the meeting was well run? You say he or she demonstrated leadership. Yes, but what *behaviors* did the manager employ that lead you to believe that the manager demonstrated leadership? Once you identify the behavior, then you can model them.

You may have heard that leadership is a lot like pornography: very hard to define, but you'll know it when you see it. The same is true for most important managerial concepts that are recognizable when you see them in action but difficult to operationalize in the abstract. Paying attention to the behaviors that support our interpretations of situations is the basis for learning how to manage. Experience is the key to deconstructing managerial concepts.

Movies, biographies, novels, and cases are another way to gather vicarious experience. To see authoritarian leadership with all its advantages and disadvantages watch George C. Scott in *Patton*, or for a look at *laissez faire* leadership see *Ghandi*. Richard Russo's *Empire Falls* illustrates business decision-making based on irrational personal motives rather than rational impersonal calculations. Jim Doig's set of biographical sketches of public sector managers, *Leadership and Innovation*, describes what these leaders did and to some extent how they did it. Activities that you may have pursued for relaxation purposes also play an important role in your managerial education. Vicarious experience gained from novels, movies, theater, and the like illustrate behaviors that support the important concepts associated with management.

This brings us to the next point. Experience, real or vicarious, is best internalized if it is processed through the brain. The processing component of this exercise is best accomplished with help. Karl Weich uses this quote to emphasize that a social environment helps organize thinking: "How do I know what I think if I do not hear what I say?" Discussing the experience is always helpful in incorporating the behavior or skill into your repertoire of experiences. We call this the linkage between beer-drinking and managerial education, although we readily admit that almost any beverage will work. Sitting and talking about an experience in an informal setting helps you claim the behavior or skill as your own. Talking about real managerial behaviors with the individual whom you are watching, or with someone else observing the behavior, brings the added advantage of possibly providing you with an understanding that would be invisible otherwise. Talking about a movie or a book allows you to probe the rationales, reexamine the behaviors, and clarify your perspective on what you saw or read. Management education can be fun.

Case studies are extremely helpful in gaining vicarious experience because they target managerial situations and put you in the position of deciding what to do and how to do it. Case studies offer a chance to play out the different scenarios possible in a problematic situation, decide what to do, look at what others would do in the same situation, and get feedback on the decision. The thinking behind your decision will be available to you later when a similar situation appears on the job. Cases analyzed and discussed in the classroom can be a marvelous way to expand vicarious experience and thus a great way to further your education as a manager.

Case Studies and Vicarious Experience

Case studies are a way to gain vicarious experience in a classroom setting. By analyzing the cases, reviewing your answers in class, examining the expert answers, and thinking through alternative strategies, you will be in a stronger position when a similar problem lands on your desk in the future. Our experience with group case reports is that students are surprised that there are many different primary problems and consequently different strategies for most cases. But this is the point. Managerial problems can be manipulated because they are subjectively defined.

People interpret events through the prism of their own experiences and their training. Living in another country and experiencing life there is one way to develop the ability to see the world as seen by other nationalities. Real experience is a potent teacher, but not many of us actually get a chance to immerse ourselves in another culture. These cases offer an alternative. The students can gain vicarious experience through situational experiences that are set in foreign countries. Vicarious experience is also a mighty teacher because it offers the student a look at life as it is lived by those inhabiting the geography of the case. These cases, although brief, offer a feel of the country, a view of the role of government in society, and a glimpse of the value structure of the country. Fiction has always been a transporter that takes the reader to another place. As teachers, we can harness that flight and use it to produce better global managers.

In these cases we see that so much of human interaction is the same; the emotions, the longings, and the relationships are common to us all. The issues administrators confront in these cases are universal as well: discrimination, accountability, transparency, and ethics. Our goal with case analysis is to expand your repertoire of behaviors. The more problematic situations you face from a managerial point of view, the more complex your thinking will become. Complex problems demand complex responses—and accumulating experiences, both real and vicarious, will help make you a more thoughtful and insightful manager.

Expanding your background of experience is the key to becoming a better manager.

Case Analysis

In our opinion, a good case should generate vicarious experience by asking you to deal with an ambiguous managerial situation and to grapple with identifying the problem and deciding on a way to solve it. We believe that managerial (not technical) problems are in the eye of the beholder. A problem is only a problem if it is articulated as such by someone who is in a position to get that problem on the action agenda. Otherwise it is an issue that exists below the radar; it is a problem only to the person who is grappling with it, invisible to those who are uninvolved. For example, some managers will believe that beginning the work day at a set time is extremely important to the efficient operation of the workplace and will punish those who are tardy. Another manager is unconcerned about a timely beginning to the workday as long as the contractual hours are met and the work gets done. Same situation—different managers—different problems.

So, the first task in case analysis is to identify the problems in the situation. A good analyst will list all the problems that he or she observes, even if the particular problem cannot be solved. (Societal racism may be a problem in a case and it is highly unlikely that you will solve that in your analysis—but it is better to be aware of it as a problem because it may influence your solutions.) Since problems are subjectively defined, there will not be a definitive list of all the problems in a given case.

Next, we recommend that you pick a problem that you want to address and that can be solved. This is the primary problem—it is the problem you intend to solve. The primary problem should be directly addressed in the solution. If it is not, then you should either change the problem or change the solution. Looping between primary problem and strategy is what a good manager does. If you like the strategy but it doesn't fit the problem, then change the problem. If you like the problem but are unhappy with the strategy, then reshape your strategy. Managerial decision-making is not a linear process. There is nothing wrong with working backwards from what appears to be an appropriate strategy.

Matching the problem and the strategy ensure that the class (or your office) understands where you are going with your strategy. Implementation is easier if you are clear about what it is you want to solve and how you plan to solve it. A good strategy takes care of the primary problem, and a better strategy includes some of the secondary problems in the plan. This is why it is good to make an extensive list of secondary problems: If you have an extensive list to look at, then it is more likely that some of the secondary problems will be included in the solution.

As instructors, our concern is that (a) the primary problem and the strategy match (clarity) and (b) some of the secondary problems are addressed in the strategy (completeness). There is no correct primary problem, although some problems cry out more for a solution than others. Julia Childs, the famous TV chef, in the early days of live television dropped a steak on the floor as she was preparing to cook it. She bent down, picked it up, brushed it off and tossed it in the pan. She leaned into the camera and said, "Honey, when you're in the kitchen, you're all alone." This applies to managerial decision-making: When you are at your desk deciding what to do about a work situation, honey, you're all alone. The choice of problem is your call. You determine how you are going to frame the problem, and your strategy for resolving the problem is based on your framing.

Global Perspective

We believe that it is a small world after all, and the excellent manager is able to see problems from many different perspectives. In this spirit, we have tried to gather cases for this book that illustrate problems that can be found anywhere in the world. Sometimes the topics in the cases may seem, at first, very foreign to an American audience. Mark Swilling's case about redevelopment policies in South Africa may appear to be a problem only of developing countries. However, upon closer examination, the problems raised in the case can happen anywhere; coping with the unintended consequences of policy decisions is a problem of governments throughout the world.

In a globalized economy, new managers will need to be able to look for similarities and differences in the unfamiliar managerial environment. And new managers are advantaged by developing a sensitivity to national and cultural differences. A fine way to gain this sensitivity is actual experience: traveling and interacting with people who are different from you. But since not many of us have the opportunity to immerse ourselves in another culture, much less many other cultures, vicarious experience is the key to cultural understanding. The cases are meant to provide the opportunity to experience problem identification and decision-making in a cultural context.

In addition to selecting cases that illustrate universal managerial and policy themes, we have organized a group of experts who give their interpretation of the situation and their recommendations for remediation. The experts were selected because they have expertise and experience and they have a global perspective. The responders were asked to identify first what is wrong in the particular case and then give the main character advice on what ought to be done. We asked three different experts to respond to each of the cases. We defined expert as someone who works or teaches in the area that is the focus of the case. We thought that because we selected reviewers from around the world, their responses would reflect that diversity. However, although we have a diversity among our responses to case situations, we are not sure that the diversity is a direct function of culture. Sometimes, we think that it is and other times we are unsure. Overall, the case responses reflect different thinking about the case situations, and as insight into different conceptions of problems and a different solution set, the case respondents fulfill their purpose. They see the case through the filter of their own experience and background. Their responses will give you a context to interpret your own case analysis. We suggest you use the three case analyses to supplement your original thinking about the case and use their ideas and suggestions to improve your own analysis.

References

Doig, J. (Ed.). (1990). *Leadership and innovation*. Baltimore: Johns Hopkins University Press.

Russo, R. (2002). *Empire falls*. New York: Vintage.

Weich, K. (1995). *Sensemaking in organizations*. Thousand Oaks, CA: Sage.

Case Study Matrix

We developed the following matrix to help you organize and think about the cases. The list of topics that appears on the vertical axis is in no way all-inclusive, but does provide a conceptual overview of the issues addressed in the cases. Each case addresses several topics and reflects the reality that managerial problems are in the eye of the beholder. We don't want this matrix to limit your use of the cases, yet we do want to provide a structure that will help you select cases.

Case Study Matrix

	Careers	Citizen participation	Communication	Conflict	Ethics	Friendships	Gender issues	Job turnover	Loyalty
Workplace of Doom				•	•				
Mixing Friends and Jobs	•					•		•	•
Starting a New Job	•								
Getting the Staff On Board			•	•					
Training Grant Decisions									
Moving Up in the Organization	•					•		•	•
Office Romance					•	•	•		•
Getting Support for Good Works			•	•					
Computer Problems at the Library									
Returning Home to Serve	•								
Reporting Local News		•	•	•					
Redevelopment & the Community		•		•	•				
University Games				•	•	•	•		•
Price of Rebuilding				•					•
Performance Reports			•						
Community Outreach Chaos		•	•	•					
Educating the Police Commissioner			•						
Parking Tickets and School Bonds		•			•				

	Media	Motivation	Nonprofit organizations	Organization politics	Organizational change	Organizational culture	Organizational evaluation
Workplace of Doom		•		•		•	
Mixing Friends and Jobs		•					
Starting a New Job					•	•	
Getting the Staff On Board		•			•	•	
Training Grant Decisions		•	•		•		•
Moving Up in the Organization		•		•	•		
Office Romance				•			
Getting Support for Good Works			•				
Computer Problems at the Library					•		
Returning Home to Serve		•		•	•	•	
Reporting Local News	•			•			•
Redevelopment & the Community			•	•	•	•	•
University Games				•	•		
Price of Rebuilding			•		•		
Performance Reports	•						•
Community Outreach Chaos	•		•				
Educating the Police Commissioner	•				•		•
Parking Tickets and School Bonds	•						

	Performance measurement	Personnel evaluations	Public policy	Public-private cooperation	Supervision	Teams
Workplace of Doom		●			●	
Mixing Friends and Jobs		●				
Starting a New Job						
Getting the Staff On Board					●	●
Training Grant Decisions			●	●		
Moving Up in the Organization		●			●	
Office Romance					●	
Getting Support for Good Works	●			●	●	
Computer Problems at the Library					●	●
Returning Home to Serve						
Reporting Local News	●					
Redevelopment & the Community	●		●	●		
University Games		●				
Price of Rebuilding			●	●		
Performance Reports	●		●		●	
Community Outreach Chaos				●		
Educating the Police Commissioner		●		●		
Parking Tickets and School Bonds						

PART I

Cases

1

Parking Tickets and School Bonds

Suzanne J. Piotrowski

The *Madison Post* is the local hometown newspaper. Hometown may be a bit of a misnomer since Madison City is a municipality with a quarter of a million people. Maria Gurule has worked as a reporter at the *Madison Post* for 15 years and for the past 10 has concentrated on city management concerns and local politics. Monday morning at 8:30 Maria rings Patricia Stoltz, the public affairs officer for Madison City.

The conversation is friendly. Maria and Patricia have known each other for more than 5 years. Maria quickly gets to the point of her call. "I understand Madison City's Office of the Treasurer has a database of outstanding unpaid parking tickets. I would like to get a copy of the database."

Patricia asks, "Would you formalize your request by writing a letter asking for the database?" Patricia knows she is required to respond to Maria within 5 business days of receiving a written request. She reminds Maria, "Legally I have five days to respond to your request. I can let you know more on Friday. Most likely I'll have the data for you then."

An intern from the *Madison Post* drops off the formal request letter later that day.

It was going to be a hectic Monday for Patricia. The day would end with a meeting on the upcoming school bond referendum chaired by the city manager, Harry Gersh. Madison City schools require major capital expenditures to be brought up to code. A similar bond referendum was defeated narrowly last year. Both Patricia and Harry feel that with some good community outreach the referendum will pass. A town meeting on the subject is scheduled for next week. Harry, Patricia, and the entire school board will be there. Patricia hopes this year the referendum will pass.

It isn't until 11 A.M. on Tuesday that Patricia reads over Maria's request letter and starts to operationalize the task. She walks down the hall to the treasurer's office and asks the deputy treasurer about the database. Indeed there is one and it is enormous. A quick review shows that there are more than 5,000 outstanding parking tickets from the past 5 years alone. Many of the outstanding tickets are from the past 3 months, so while they are technically overdue, the offenders still could pay the tickets with just a small penalty. The database also includes the home addresses, phone numbers, and personal identifiers of the individuals who own the cars that were ticketed.

Patricia calls Maria on her cell phone that afternoon. "Could you give me a better idea of what you are looking for?" asks Patricia. "The database includes an enormous number of outstanding tickets, some of which are newly issued. Also, the file includes personal identifiers and I am not even sure if all the information is releasable."

Maria responds, "Really, I am just looking for big-time offenders. If you give me a list of everyone who owes more than $250 in parking tickets that would satisfy my request. Also, I only really need their names and addresses." Since Maria had made information requests before, she knew her right to receive the database in electronic form.

The two chat for a few more minutes when Maria offers the impetus for the request. A neighboring municipality had similar information published, and it turned out some local business owners were racking up huge parking ticket bills and never paying them. Maria was interested if she would find the same. She intended to post the dataset on the *Madison Post*'s Web site.

Wednesday morning Patricia consults the city's attorney, and Maria was correct. She could receive the information in electronic form. Also, there are no restrictions on what a person could do with government documents once they are released. Maria could legally post the information on the Web site. The dataset would have to be redacted, though, in order to release the requested information without the personal identifiers such as social security numbers.

The city's attorney makes it clear that the release of these data would violate individuals' right to privacy. The attorney also states that "Madison City is only obligated to incur *reasonable costs* in the process of making documents available for release. Reasonable cost isn't defined, though. You just need to use your best judgment."

Patricia thinks that redacting the database wouldn't take more than a day of labor, and this is a reasonable cost. Patricia has always considered herself an advocate of transparency. She can't see any reason not to release the dataset. Anyway, Maria had piqued her interest. Whose names would be on the list?

Again Patricia walks down the hall to the treasurer's office. She is told that the job will take at least 2 full days of work and will probably be completed by Friday around noon. Patricia still thinks that this is a reasonable cost and asks that the treasurer's office go ahead with the project. She tells the deputy treasurer, "There may be some interesting names on this list. Let me know if anyone of note pops up."

Friday is another busy day for Patricia. She has a 4 P.M. appointment planned with the town manager to prepare for next Wednesday's meeting on the bond referendum. She knows Maria will be calling this afternoon as well. While she doesn't have to produce the database today, she needs to let her know when it will be available.

She checks in with the deputy treasurer.

The database is almost ready for release, but there are still a couple more hours of work that need to be done. Unfortunately, the person who is working on the database has Friday afternoons off. It will have to be finished on Monday. Patricia then inquires if after looking through the database any local business owners' names were on the list. The deputy treasurer explains, "I didn't see any local business owners, but there were a few surprises. Three of the school board members have outstanding tickets totaling over $250. One actually owes $1,100! So far there are a few other city officials on the list too."

Patricia walks away in a bit of shock. If this information got out, it would probably derail the school bond referendum. She could see next week's town meeting focusing on the unpaid parking tickets, not the much needed school repairs. What should she do? Did another few hours of work count as unreasonable costs? The majority of the project was already completed, though. The dataset would be ready on Monday. Should she release the information before the town meeting? Could she wait and release it at the end of next week after the meeting? She will see Harry that afternoon. Should she ask the city manager what to do? Would this be getting him involved unnecessarily?

Patricia has 3 hours to decide. She has to respond to Maria by 5 P.M. today.

Suzanne J. Piotrowski teaches public administration at Rutgers University–Campus at Newark. She specializes in freedom of information policy and practice.

2

The Education of
the Police Commissioner

Erwin Schwella

To varying degrees, crime threatens all nations, but new democracies are
particularly vulnerable. As reported in the media, the country was infested
with a crime wave that put ordinary citizens behind security bars while the
criminals were seemingly celebrating their perverted view of liberation by
roaming free while performing murder, rape, robbery, and carjacking as
well as many more seemingly petty nonviolent crimes such as fraud, theft,
corruption, and the like. Criminality was threatening to also steal and
embezzle the highly valued and hard-earned freedom from the majority of
ordinary law-abiding citizens.

Crime is a problem for the police, but the organization of the police
had been a major issue from the beginning since some elements of the
police force were active in the suppression of the democratic forces. It was
therefore not surprising that the majority of citizens who were part of the
liberation struggle feared and resented the police. The country's new constitution included serious mechanisms to make the police politically
accountable and subject to government and civilian oversight. Also, it
was decided to create a totally new and integrated leadership structure.
The 11 previous police entities were integrated into a single police service
consisting of 160,000 individuals from diverse national organizational
and ethnic cultures. Everything from values, policies, and strategies
through uniforms, ranks, and language usage had to be changed simultaneously. Given all this change, it is not difficult to understand why the

suicide rates and incidence of alcohol dependency as well as absenteeism among police officers soared. Within the police force there were continuous claims of racism from all sides, amplified by a process of affirmative action that had to be introduced for all the right reasons but was seen as either too little too late or as reverse discrimination premised upon revenge based on political interference.

The president was keenly aware that something had to be done. He needed a highly successful leader, someone with a proven track record. Mr. Mayerbeer, chief executive of the National African Brewery (NAB) fit the bill. NAB was a success story even during the old regime and it was moving quickly to fit in the new democracy. Soon after the advent of democracy, NAB made bold moves in the area of black empowerment and appointed black directors and senior staff. NAB also supported worthy and politically sound causes of the Newsa government. With the opening up of international business opportunities, NAB moved fast, and a series of transactions followed leading to a London listing and a spot in the FTSE 100 index for NAB and an escalation of status to the second largest brewery company in the world.

In NAB, applying sound business principles worked for shareholders, owners, directors, and the consumers—in large quantities of quality products such as Bastion beer, which also continued to be popular with almost all the members of the police irrespective of their background. The taste and effects of NAB products may even sometimes have been one of the few shared experiences of the highly diverse members of the National Police Force (NPF) during their days facing difficult transitions and transformation. In any case, by all standards NAB was a hugely successful, well-managed company following sound business principles to enhance its success.

The leadership of NAB was a major contributor to the success of the company. Mr. Mayerbeer succeeded in the face of adversity where others would probably have failed. When opportunities arose after the changes in the country, he even exceeded his previous performance and he was generally known as the leading industrialist and a top business leader with wisdom, zeal, and passion. He was highly regarded also for his warm personality, straight-talking honesty, and great sense of humor. He was reported also to have an affinity for a good fight, but with a solid capacity to let bygones be bygones and to concentrate on the business at hand after being extremely frank and direct. During his career he was quite used to laying down the law and getting his way in the interest of reaching challenging organizational goals and objectives. Henry Mayerbeer was a man who got things done.

It was a late summer's day in March 1997 when Henry Mayerbeer's personal assistant interrupted a board meeting that he was attending after knocking and entering the austere board room filled with very businesslike people. The personal assistant said, in an apologetic way, "Chair, I am really sorry to interrupt the meeting as I realize that the board has issued clear instructions that board meetings should only be interrupted under the most pressing urgent circumstances. However, I have the Office of the President on the line with a request that the president would like to speak to Mr. Mayerbeer urgently. I hope board members will understand." At this point Mr. Mayerbeer was already on his way to take the call in his office, where the following conversation took place:

"Good afternoon, Mr. President," said Mr. Mayerbeer.

The well-known, polite voice of the president was on the other end of the line. "Hello, Mr. Mayerbeer. I do appreciate your willingness to talk to me when, from what I hear, you are busy with an important meeting. This is, however, a matter of national importance. Do you mind if I get straight to the point?"

"Of course not, Mr. President. I realize what extreme work-related pressures you are under, as am I, so please go ahead."

"You will know that the government is, like the rest of the country, seriously concerned about the crime situation in the country. At the last couple of cabinet meetings all aspects of this worrying state of affairs were discussed in depth. It was realized that, among other things, the effectiveness of the National Police Force impacts on the handling of crime in the country. There are concerns about the state of management in the NPF due to a number of very complex factors. It was then decided that we should approach you to ascertain whether you would be willing to help in this regard—"

"Crime is one of the gravest issues faced by business as well," a surprised Mayerbeer interrupted politely, "and we realize the importance of the NPF in dealing with this, but I am not sure how I can assist from my position here at NAB."

"We are being even more, hmm, challenging than that and thought that the situation may require a really bold strategy. To be brief, we were wondering whether you, with the cooperation of NAB, would be willing to become the chief executive officer of the NPF, for a period of 24 to 36 months. Wait, wait, before you react immediately, we know this is a tall order, but we have huge respect for the patriotism of you yourself and NAB as a company. Your country really needs you now and we want to really plead with you to consider this in the interest of all our people. We need your leadership and business competencies to improve the management of the NPF for the benefit of the country. If you would consider this we also have to move fast. If the idea is not totally out of line, I would like to set up a meeting with you toward the end of next week to take the matter further. May I suggest that you think about this and discuss it privately with stakeholders and that we then meet to consider the matter further?"

"Mr. President, I am of course honored by your commending words, but you will realize what you are requesting will have many personal and professional consequences for me, the NAB and the NPF. I shall appreciate meeting you, but will only be able to give you an indication of my answer in this regard after consideration and consultation. I hope you will understand. . . ."

"Of course, but I shall really be greatly appreciative if you and NAB can assist our beautiful country in this way. I look forward to a positive answer from you when we meet next week. Will it be OK if my office sets up such a meeting at the presidency when it suits us both, but not later than Friday next week?"

Mr. Mayerbeer knew he was neatly roped in, and in some ways he found the possibility to make a positive contribution challenging and exciting. It would not in any way be easy and simple, but then again neither was life, or successfully managing a globally operating and competitive business conglomerate. He reacted: "Till our meeting then, Mr. President. As I have said, I am honored by your confidence. Good-bye and thank you."

The Meeting

At the meeting, which took place the next week as arranged, Henry Mayerbeer was in a position, after proper consultation, to agree to the President's request. It was decided that he would become the CEO of the NPF for an initial period of 24 months, after which the position could be reconsidered. He would assume duty on a part-time basis during July 1997 and would take real office for the period on August 1. He was given a broad mandate to assist in making the NPF an effective, successful organization using his expertise and competencies. He was to be in charge of the police budget and would manage all the human and physical resources of the NPF.

One Year Later

During an interview with a prominent Sunday newspaper, the *Sunday News*, exactly a year after assuming office Mr. Mayerbeer was clearly on the defensive. The report started by suggesting that Mr. Mayerbeer should tidy his desk at the NPF head office and go, as after his first year the country was still torn apart by crime. Mr. Mayerbeer's reaction to this is described in the report in the following way: "In fact, the combustible chief of NAB comes close to a liftoff when the possibility of his departure is suggested." According to the report, he thinks that he has done superbly, but that the optimism still has to filter through to the ground, where it ultimately matters. He also does not see himself as Mr. Crimebuster but as a management man, who has to lay foundations, change structures, and alter mindsets. The reporter confronted the CEO with the results of a number of independent researchers. These researchers found that many police stations still functioned without pens, paper, and patrol cars, that red tape was as stifling as always, and that manpower was spread as unevenly as in the past. In reaction to these findings Mr. Mayerbeer used some classical defenses such as

- "For some researcher to go out into the *bundu* and come back with criticism about managing the police service is fairly offensive. When I die, I want to come back as an independent researcher."
- "Until you teach that area commissioner what to do with those requisition forms . . . I wish you could find me some effectiveness and efficiency and honesty pills. We'd spend our whole budget on them."
- "They're still making too many mistakes, that's a fact. We haven't gone from where we were to glory overnight."
- "Why don't I bring in a number of high-fliers from the private sector to take this machine and redo it overnight? That's naiveté of the worst kind. The minute we move out, the whole thing will collapse."

Mr. Mayerbeer also stressed that everything he had to implement had to be simple, affordable, and workable so that it could be taken over by the current level of NPF management. It also had to be painstakingly negotiated every inch of the way. In fact, for the first 3 months into the first year of taking office, nothing happened except negotiation and consultation.

The Second Year

The second year was, from all accounts just as hard. After this year Mr. Mayerbeer announced that he would not renew his contract. According to reports, he added that the police were losing the battle against crime. Although the NPF management had a plan to combat crime and was qualified to implement it, he doubted whether they had the resources to implement it.

Subsequent to this announcement Mr. Mayerbeer was convinced by the political leaders to stay on for 6 more months, but thereafter he left and rejoined the NAB in a senior executive position in London, England. The final question to consider is to evaluate the success of Mr. Mayerbeer in his quest to manage toward a turnaround in the NPF. By all standards his departure attracted much less attention than his arrival.

He had just spent 2 years and 6 months of his life trying to do his best for the country and people he loves. There were successes. A new detective academy had been established that was showing promise in the training of detectives. There were indications that the established Anti-Corruption Unit was encouraging the uncovering of corruption, but the irony was that this created the perception that corruption was even more prevalent than alleged. He felt that he had made some impact on improving the redistribution of human and other resources from police stations in the previously advantaged areas to stations in the high-crime, previously disadvantaged areas.

Then again, for all the hard-won management improvements, the crime statistics were disconcerting, as there were indications of significant increases in some serious crime areas. He wondered over the impact of management improvements on the crime situation and was puzzled by the seeming lack of impact the management improvements had on crime-combating results. If he had effected similar changes in the processes of the brewery, he was sure he would have had created much improved results on the profit bottom line of the company. How could the lack of clearly visible results be explained? What could he have done differently? As an analytical and results-oriented man he was going to grapple with these questions.

He wanted to consider what he could learn from the experience and what he would write in his final report to the NPF management.

Erwin Schwella is the director of the department of public management and planning at the University of Stellenbosch, South Africa.

3

Community Outreach Chaos

Kathryn Hammond

Dr. Janet Schuman was thrilled when Montville College was awarded a large grant from the National Metropolitan Development Agency (MDA) to develop a Community Outreach Partnership Center (COPC). COPC grants assist colleges and universities in providing technical assistance, training, and applied research to address the expressed needs of urban communities. It strives to take advantage of the knowledge and enthusiasm of students, faculty, and community partners to mobilize the assets *within* and *between* the campus and community.

While preparing the grant proposal, Dr. Schuman paid careful attention to all of the specified guidelines in the request for proposal. Universities and colleges are required to define and describe a target area (or urban community) via census tracts and other reliable data sources. Urban areas must have a minimum of 2,500 residents. Proposed projects should match the initiatives of MDA while tapping the resources of the university or college. The residents themselves should identify community needs. Funds are awarded to the institution of higher education and cannot be paid directly to citizens during implementation. All COPC applicants are required to have written support from the organizations and local governments with which they partner.

While gearing up to write the proposal, Dr. Schuman sought the support of the town mayor and council to meet some of the MDA requirements. She was pleased when the mayor suggested that one of the councilmen appoint a steering committee of local leaders and activists to help identify neighborhood needs and the strategies to address them.

Dr. Schuman rounded out the steering committee with members of the college who were committed to undertaking this kind of community-based project. During their first meeting, the steering committee spent a significant amount of time discussing the grant, its parameters, and the critical issues of the neighborhood it would address.

The Elm Street neighborhood seemed the appropriate target area for the grant proposal. It was an enclave that residents thought of as a "community within a community," with characteristics separate and distinct from other sections of Montville. When taken as a whole, Montville is well known as a relatively prosperous town serving as a national model of diversity and integration. Much of the African American population, however, is concentrated in and around the Elm Street neighborhood. In more detail, the target neighborhood consisted of all of census tract 16 of the Township of Montville. Tract 16 has a population of 2,794 in an area of 0.3 square mile, with 2,298 African American residents and 496 white residents. The median household income of the Elm Street neighborhood is $25,658 (an income dramatically lower than the median household income of $74,588 of the larger Montville).

Intensifying the stark disparities exhibited between the Elm Street neighborhood and the larger Montville was the construction of the "Montville Link," a rail connection offering a direct ride to a major metropolitan city. Making room for the rail line called for ongoing construction and the demolition of 19 houses in the Elm Street enclave, with the displacement of 27 families. In addition, 48 housing units were vacant and would remain so until the completion of the Montville Link, at which time rent was expected to increase significantly, reaching far beyond the means of many neighborhood residents.

Dr. Schuman felt confident that the Census Bureau data and transportation developments clearly pointed to a community in need. She and her colleagues feverishly began the process of designing projects that included hosting workshops highlighting the rights and responsibilities of landlords and tenants and neighborhood forums to foster linkages among residents to address local needs. Community members of the steering committee reviewed the proposal before submission. Most seemed pleased with the result and agreed to work on the project in the event it was funded. The group disbanded, awaiting the funding decision of MDA.

The time had finally arrived for the proposed activities to be put into action. After funding, a majority of Dr. Schuman's work as the COPC director involved organizing resources and reorienting her team to the proposed activities and timetable for implementation. The funding received local coverage in the *Montville Record*, a popular weekly town newspaper. Headlines emphasized the sizable $400,000 grant awarded to Montville College. A majority of the accolades went to the mayor and college administration. Steering committee members and community partners were not highlighted in the articles. Although Dr. Schuman was not particularly pleased with this oversight, she assumed the good work of the COPC team would become the central theme of future headlines and stories. Such optimism, however, would not quell the grumbles among well-known community residents and activists. Although some of the steering committee members and residents called Dr. Schuman to voice their concerns, she still pushed forward with arrangements for the upcoming workshops and neighborhood forums.

A workshop for tenants was the first of the COPC activities to be implemented. Montville faculty presented information to residents covering landlord/tenant rights and responsibilities. Dr. Schuman was disappointed when only four residents attended. She had concentrated on an extensive outreach effort that included a flyer mailing and newspaper announcements. A reporter for the *Montville Record* was present and recounted the abysmal attendance in an article titled "Renters are a No-Show at First COPC Sponsored Workshop." The low resident turnout and newspaper coverage launched a campuswide buzz. Dr. Schuman's colleagues warned that this kind of negative coverage would lead to a backlash from college administration. The college, after all, had spent a number of years engaging and developing partnerships with organizations in the community.

Resident attendance, however, didn't seem to be a problem for the subsequent Neighborhood Forum. Contrary to the scarce turnout at the recent workshop, this event was crowded with residents, local activists and leaders, COPC team members, college faculty, and students.

Dr. Schuman and her COPC colleagues were informally introducing themselves to the residents. Yet rather than breaking the ice and discussing ways to work together on community issues, residents outwardly expressed their reservation about the project. It was clear a core group branded the COPC efforts as patronizing and ill equipped to handle the *real* needs of the community.

Some directly questioned Dr. Schuman as to how their Elm Street neighborhood was selected as the "targeted area." Others, such as Rhonda Howard, a well-respected and often outspoken activist wanted to know why she wasn't chosen to be part of the steering committee. She asked some other attendants in a voice loud enough to be heard by many at the session, "How are these college professors and their naïve students supposed to solve our problems? They probably got lost getting here tonight while they were coming down from the college on the hill."

Frank Jerome, the president of the Montville chapter of the National Association for the Advancement of Colored People (NAACP) was questioning who was getting paid from the grant funds, and why the COPC team did not reflect the diversity of the town. There was a sign-up sheet circulating the room prompting folks to join an ad hoc committee to investigate the COPC. Meanwhile the local reporter was interviewing residents and taking pictures for the next edition of the *Montville Record*.

In the midst of this chaos, Dr. Schuman had to compose herself, for she was just about to move to the podium to introduce the project and the evening's activities. She walked up to the podium and looked upon angry faces. She saw the local reporter with pen and paper in hand. As she began to greet the participants, the NAACP president interrupted her. The first of a battery of questions was coming her way. How was she going to address them in a way that would represent the good intentions of the COPC project? But more importantly, what was she going to do tomorrow?

Kathryn Hammond ran a Community Outreach Partnership in New Jersey and is currently pursuing a PhD in Public Administration at Rutgers University–Campus at Newark.

4

Performance Reports

Karel van der Molen and Belinda Van Wyk

Alfred Ndlovu, the municipal manager of Sunnyview for the past 2 years, just emerged from a long meeting with his senior management team. The meeting was intended to structure a report on the performance of the municipality over the past quarter. The report must be presented to the regional council by the end of the month.

At the meeting, the head of each service area was asked to report on their activities and achievements. All of the service area managers reported that they were doing their best within the limited budgets available to them. Some indicated that the shortage of employees and the large number of vacancies that had not been filled had affected their performance.

"The high turnover in staff has really threatened our ability to provide quality services. We are really strapped," complained the head of public works.

The human resource manager responded and agreed that it was hard to keep a full complement of staff. "I think the larger municipalities and private businesses are poaching many of our experienced staff members. They offer higher wages and more comprehensive benefits and we can't compete."

Mr. Ndlovu outlined a series of issues he felt needed some thought. He noted that a number of critical issues had been raised by the press. In addition, citizens have been complaining about the poor quality of service delivery in several critical areas. Some of the issues raised included high levels of child abuse and the lack of government-subsidized housing. Sunnyview also experienced an increase in crime over the past year.

"With so many people out of work we have witnessed an increase in petty thefts and burglaries" the police chief stated. "While the crime rate has increased—and believe me we are concerned about that—personal safety has not been threatened."

On top of the rising crime rate and the increase in child abuse, there had also been a report that a housing project had been delayed for months because of the inadequate infrastructure for water and electricity. The local paper ran an article that was quite negative that included comments and pictures of people who said the municipality was failing them.

There was significant disagreement among the senior management team. Some members felt that Mr. Ndlovu should report that Sunnyview had been quite successful under the circumstances. They felt so much had been accomplished in the past quarter. They did not feel that the negative media coverage and a few complaints from a handful of citizens were an accurate reflection of their accomplishments. When Mr. Ndlovu questioned whether they should really paint such an optimistic picture, it led to a heated discussion.

"The murder rate is down, so is the number of reported rapes," argued the police chief. "Why can't we just report that and leave out the data on the increased burglaries?"

The human resource manager wanted to focus on the poaching of experienced staff members.

During the heated debate other problems were uncovered. It appeared that bureaucratic delays in obtaining approval for expenditures on project changes created big problems. Garbage could not be collected in some places because the high levels of crime made it too dangerous. Squatters from the township were illegally occupying almost 800 housing units. To solve this situation, a long process of negotiation and reallocation of housing facilities is needed, but this will only create more delays and aggravate the community further. The senior management team agreed that Sunnyview was doing the best it could to address the growing problems they faced. They also agreed that more needed to be done to ensure safety and improve the quality of life. What they could not agree on was how to present their quarterly performance to the regional council.

Mr. Ndlovu adjourned the meeting realizing the team would not be able to reach consensus on the report. It was up to him as the municipal manager to determine what to report to the council. The previous manager's reports never discussed internal or external problems, but clearly, the problems being confronted by Sunnyview are not new to Mr. Ndlovu's administration. His senior staff reminded him during the meeting that political interference and organizational politics was a major concern. They let him know that the elected officials seemed more interested in laying blame than solving problems. Mr. Ndlovu has his work cut out. He has a lot of performance data, but the question is how to present those data to the regional council.

Karel van der Molen is a professional associate of Unistel-Consultus and teaches at the University of Stellenbosch, South Africa.

Belinda Van Wyk is a lecturer at the University of Stellenbosch.

5

The Price of Rebuilding a War-Torn Town

Bojana Blagojevic

Maria's nongovernmental organization has operated in a small war-torn town for years. They assisted the local people and shared their struggle to survive in the midst of constant fighting, shelling, hunger, and despair. One year has passed since the war ended. Finally, there is electricity and running water, and a hope for the future has returned to the war-shattered place. Maria has been the director of the organization since the outset of the war. During the war, her organization's main goal was to provide emergency medical aid and food. Even though the humanitarian needs are still present, the time has come to refocus the work on postconflict development by helping people heal and rebuild their lives. At a recent meeting, Maria and her coworkers decided that the new priorities for the organization would be providing economic assistance and promoting inter-ethnic reconciliation through refugee returns.

At the staff meeting, one of the colleagues pointed out a perfect economic assistance project. A major source of employment in the town, a furniture factory, was completely destroyed during the war. As a result, the majority of the town population became jobless. Everyone in the organization agrees that rebuilding the factory would be an appropriate development project and a necessary step in rebuilding this war-ravaged town. Thanks to the high level of coverage by the international media and the organization's public relations department, donors were very generous in providing the funds for postconflict assistance. The decision of the best way to put the funds to use has not come solely from within the organization. One hundred and fifty families were interviewed and asked what they believed would be most helpful in rebuilding their lives. The overwhelming majority agreed that the best way to help would be to create jobs and revive the halted economy. Poverty and unemployment, all agreed, are the biggest problems. Ivana, who lives near Maria's office, said in the interview, "My biggest wish is to work again. I was always able to provide for my family— I worked as a cook before the war. Now I feel helpless, because there is no job for me. I would work anywhere, just to be a productive person again. The feeling of helplessness is killing me." Most of the interviewed people expressed their desire to see the factory rebuilt, believing that the jobs it would create would bring the town back to life.

Another consideration that came at the top of the agenda was return and reconciliation of the refugees. A recent report by the United Nations High Commissioner for Refugees indicated there was a large number of refugees and displaced ethnic minorities who wished to return to their homes in this town. The interviewed families were asked if they were in favor of their ethnic minority neighbors returning to their homes. About 60% of the families said it would be difficult to get along with them again, but they would try if they had to.

Since the end of the war, local politicians have done everything in their power to prevent ethnic minorities from returning to the town, and no projects could be carried out without their approval. Maria and her coworkers decided that in order to combine organizational priorities, the project of rebuilding the factory would be implemented in exchange for the return of the refugees. The hope was that an economic incentive would persuade the local government to do its part in the refugee and reconciliation effort. A colleague from the organization disagreed and warned that the inter-ethnic animosities are still fresh and that a refugee and reconciliation project should be undertaken when enough time had passed. He suggested that the current project should be limited to rebuilding the factory, in order not to alienate the local government. As the director of the organization, Maria had to make the ultimate decision. She thought about the suggestion, but decided that it is important to plant the seeds of reconciliation early after the cessation of hostilities.

Maria and her coworkers prepared the project plan and headed to meet with the leader of the town's refugee group before asking for the mayor's approval to carry out the project. At the meeting, they shared the project idea with the refugee leader, who was enthusiastic about the prospect of bringing his people home. The leader noted that that he felt concerned and uncomfortable living next to and working with the majority group, but he stressed that jobs and homes were the most important. He asked Maria's organization to be a mediator in getting the town's politicians to provide mechanisms to ensure the refugees' safety.

An appointment with the mayor was set. On their way to the mayor's office, Maria and John passed by the destroyed factory. Maria felt an enormous excitement visualizing the new factory, people returning to work, and the future of the town beginning. They soon arrived at the municipal building and the mayor greeted them warmly when they entered his office. After exchanging polite "good afternoons," the mayor said, "First of all, I would like to thank you for helping this town throughout the war. Your organization has been here with us through all of the hardships. You stood by us and we consider you to be our own people."

"Thank you," Maria replied, "We love this town and are happy to help in any way we can. We are here today because we have an idea for an exciting new project. My organization would like to help rebuild the furniture factory in exchange for allowing the ethnic minority refugees and displaced persons to return to their homes. The funds are available, and the project is ready. Your approval is all we need to begin the work."

To her dismay, after a moment of awkward silence, the mayor looked Maria straight into the eye and said, "I cannot be bought!"

"But . . ." she tried to reply.

"No 'but,' no discussion! You were here during the war. You have seen with your own eyes that their army—they—destroyed this city with shelling. Why should we allow them to come back here? This is no longer their town," the mayor said in angry excitement.

Suddenly, it dawned on Maria how little attention she paid to the ethnic hatred and intolerance factor in the situation. Perhaps they should have disregarded the reconciliation issue and proceeded only with the economic assistance. The organizational planning did not account for this kind of an obstacle. As thoughts were flying through her head, Maria realized that she did not anticipate this kind of a response from the mayor. In a last attempt, she said:

"The factory would help your town enormously. It is not a bargain. Furthermore, civilians, regardless of their ethnicity, have a right to return to their homes."

"They are all the same," the mayor maintained. "They are the enemy. Rebuild the factory, if you'd like, but no refugees! No enemies are allowed in this town."

Then he excused himself and left the room.

Immediately upon returning to their office, Maria convened a staff meeting. After a short briefing, she asked the staff to make suggestions about what should be done. Someone suggested that they go ahead and rebuild the factory and give up on the resettlement and reconciliation issue.

Others suggested involvement of other organizations and more moderate politicians in pressuring the mayor to allow the returns. Another suggestion was to carry out a similar project in another town. Maria thanked everyone for their input and informed them that she would make a decision by the next staff meeting. She thought how sad it was that there was a price for rebuilding the town's future and started thinking about different ways of approaching the problem.

Bojana Blagojevic, from Rutgers University–Campus at Newark, worked for the International Committee of the Red Cross during the war in her home country, Bosnia.

6

University Games

Helen Paxton

Alexandria was a city that captured Melissa's interest. She had worked as a marketing and communications professional in the city for 12 years and in the process had seen a lot of problems and a lot of progress. As an old city in a densely populated region, Alexandria's rich history in business, the arts, culture, and education was nowhere near as well known as its problems of declining population, housing, grime, and crime. Despite the city's image problems, there were a lot of people, including some of the region's most powerful and wealthiest citizens, who cared deeply about the city and its future.

Melissa had come to work at Northern University after many years in the city's nonprofit arts sector. There were many similarities in the work she was now doing promoting Northern U's business school to what she had done in the world of the arts. While interviewing for the position at Northern she had come to realize that the experience she had promoting the arts in the city would serve her well in higher education. Both sectors were long-time neighbors in Alexandria as in other large old cities around the world. These venerable urban institutions faced significant challenges as newer organizations in increasingly populated suburban areas gained a stronghold and became ever more competitive.

In the city of Alexandria, every organization, not just the big ones, shared the same challenges. How to promote a fine institution in a not-glamorous city. How to bring the desired customer base to the institution. How to deal with perceptions of the city as a dangerous place. How to promote the revitalization of the city without sugar-coating the reality.

After all, location is often one of the most significant factors worldwide in creating a positive image and developing an effective communications and marketing program. If Columbia University were located in Columbia,

Missouri, instead of New York City, with the same faculty and facilities, would it still be able to attract the same number of highly qualified students? If the British Museum were located in Manchester instead of London, would people be traveling from all over the world to view its collections? Institutions located in desirable locations almost always have a competitive advantage, and the ones in less attractive and especially troubled locations almost always have to contend with the ripple effect of the location on their institutional image.

Melissa wanted very much to have a larger role to play in Northern U's fortunes. She was not afraid of dealing head-on with the challenges of any organization she worked with; in fact, she had come to have a deep-seated conviction that organizations need to address their problems directly if they want to bring about change. And having worked in the city for a long time, she enjoyed promoting organizations that were often perceived as second best primarily because of their location. Too many people in communications, she felt, just swept the thorny problems under the bed, and dealt with public relations as a window dressing. And we all know that the public is way too smart to believe that window dressing comes close to telling the whole story.

The more she looked into the way Northern U was promoting itself, the more convinced she became that a better job could be done and that she would like to be a major player. The campus' director of communications, an intelligent and experienced professional who had been in that position for a number of years, ran an operation that was a bit sleepy. The office was underfunded and understaffed and didn't seem up to the job that needed to be done. Furthermore, the office seemed to be in a perpetual reactive mode. If someone asked them to help with a project, help was forthcoming. A press release here, a news story there, a publication here, an ad there. There seemed to be no overall vision or unity to the work, and the reputation of the office around campus was hardly positive, making it especially difficult to advocate for increased funding to support communications initiatives. Melissa knew that a new approach was needed.

There being no time like the present, Melissa made her move. She set up an appointment with Evan, the senior administrator responsible for oversight of the communications office.

"Thanks for meeting with me, Evan," she began. "As you know, I am concerned that the communications office isn't performing as well as they could be. They should be doing more to promote the university and the city of Alexandria."

To her delight, Evan was very interested in what she had to say and wanted to learn more.

"What do you propose that the office do differently?" Evan asked.

Melissa talked openly and honestly about her vision for the communications office and what she we do to actively promote the university. They spoke for nearly an hour and discovered they shared many of the same concerns. She ended their meeting by saying "Evan, if there is ever an opportunity for a new direction and director in the communications office, I would like to be considered."

A few days later Evan called and suggested that Melissa propose a project that would address the issues they had discussed but that it be a project she would work on with the communications director. Evan's approach caught Melissa a bit off her guard. She was intrigued and most certainly interested in going forward but was concerned that it might be an awkward way for her to work on this project. But she decided to take up the offer and proposed a print publications project that would communicate the great strengths of the university and its home city.

Within days she received a go ahead and an approved budget for her project. Evan had made it clear that if she could work successfully on this project with the present director, she would be considered for the job of taking over the office, and the present director would become a staff member reporting to her. Melissa practically floated out of the office that day, she was so excited about her new challenge and professional opportunity.

It was years ago that a business colleague jokingly said to Melissa, "Be careful what you wish for, you might just get it." These words came back to her the next day as the reality of what she had been asked to do sank in. Her head was practically spinning with unanswered questions. She was excited about the opportunity, but why would Evan put her in such a position?

After thinking long and hard about her approach, Melissa picked up the phone and called Stefan that afternoon. "Stefan, I'd like to set up a meeting to talk with you about some ideas I have for a university-wide publicity campaign. I've already shared my ideas with Evan and he suggested we work together on this initiative."

There was a long silence, and then Stefan finally spoke, somewhat hesitantly, as if searching for the right words. "I'm a bit confused as to why you would be involved in such a campaign. It seems unusual, at best, that someone outside of my office would be proposing such a thing and having discussions with my boss without my knowledge."

"Oh" was Melissa's response. "I'll stop by your office before I head home tonight." Now what was she going to say to him?

Helen Paxton is the director of campus communications at Rutgers University–Campus at Newark.

7

Redevelopment and the Community

Mark Swilling

Marconi Beam is an informal settlement that grew up in the heart of a conservative white Cape Town suburb called Milnerton. During apartheid it was continuously raided and harassed by the police, but it benefited from the democratic transition by winning official recognition and a measure of protection from the security forces and white ratepayers during post-apartheid and had grown to 3,000 people. President Nelson Mandela chose Marconi Beam to launch the *Masakhane* campaign (Let's Build Together). This was testimony to the fact that this complex settlement, with its mixed colored and Xhosa-speaking community, had become a high-profile housing development, complete with subsidies, technical plans, forums for consulting the surrounding white community, a development trust, NGO advisors, and a for-profit development company called CON-DEV. For Mandela and his entourage, this was demonstrable proof of delivery by the new democratic government, and of reconciliation between the poor black homeless people and surrounding white middle class. But the images of linear progress inscribed in the self-help prescriptions of the prevailing urban development approach belie the complexity of the actual processes on the ground.

Sipho Mpetha, a Xhosa speaker in his mid-30s, grew up in the Eastern Cape rural town of Craddock. An ANC activist and community worker, Sipho became project coordinator of an NGO job-creation program in Marconi Beam. His ability to speak Xhosa, English, and Afrikaans and his grasp of dominant development discourses enabled Sipho to gain rapid entry into the NGO world and local municipal politics. He was, however, totally dependent on largely white industrialists, developers, bureaucrats, and NGO workers for access to resources, a subordinate position he resented intensely. Referring to one powerful white industrialist he was required to work with he said, "I do not accept to be represented by somebody who is living in luxury. . . . he must come and see how I live."

Buli, however, had chosen a different road. As a militant "Young Lion" of the anti-apartheid street battles and urban wars, Buli was a *tsotsi* (gangster)—complete with scars from many knife battles, the tattoo of the famous "28" gang, ritualized smoking of the renowned Cape Town "white pipe" (a deadly mix of mandrax tablets and marijuana), and the distinctive style of walking and talking of the Cape gangs. He is in Marconi Beam because here he can disappear into an underworld that gives him access to resources and social power without having to participate in the politics of bureaucratic governance and development that requires a level of literacy, legal identity, and communicative ability that he does not possess. For him, the transformation of Marconi Beam through "development" is a threat to his way of surviving, but this is a distraction to be ducked, rather than something worth bothering to engage until such time as it threatens his anonymity or access to illegal resource flows or, indeed, his identity as a free user of urban resources.

The origins of Marconi Beam go back to apartheid when mainly homeless "colored" squatters established a settlement in *die bos* (the bush) called Cukutown. The settlement gradually expanded as Xhosa-speaking African people moved into the settlement, and soon it was composed of about 3,000 people and had been officially recognized as a development area rather than a "black spot" to be removed from white suburbia. A complex partnership between central government, local government, private-sector developers, NGOs, and community groups was established to supervise the development of the area. Twelve hundred formal houses for a slightly upscale market were constructed in an area called Phoenix, and 1,000 serviced sites, with core structures were established for the lower end of the market in an area that came to be called Joe Slovo Park, after the first housing minister of the first democratic government.

There were three settlements: Phoenix, which was inhabited by lower-middle-class white and colored residents; Slovo Park, which was inhabited by Xhosa-speaking working-class and informally employed people; and the old Cukutown, made up of about 400 shacks inhabited by a wide range of working people waiting to move into houses in Slovo Park, unemployed people with nowhere to go, the indigent old who had found a place to stay for a while, largely homeless street children, gangsters who needed the protection of informal anonymity, sex workers passing through, and a mix of traders from shop owners to shebeen (unlicensed drinking establishment) operators. The impenetrable informality of Cukutown meant that its inhabitants were able to evolve a localized urban culture within a space that was not regulated or controlled by any outside authority. However, this was temporary because the understanding that had been reached between Phoenix, the white suburbs, Slovo Park, and Cukutown residents was that as people moved from Cukutown into the Slovo Park houses, their shacks would be demolished, leading, eventually, to the complete eradication of informal housing in the area.

It was a plan that suited the nonracial vision of the old and new entrants to urban modernity: For the whites, property prices would return to their old levels once the shacks were gone and the new areas absorbed into suburban culture; for the coloreds, having their "own place" in suburbia was more than enough, and once Cukutown was gone, the shebeens, gangsters, and prostitutes would move out; and for the Africans who were moving into Slovo Park, for some this was the realization of a long promised urban dream, but for others it meant having to find the funds to pay the bond repayments and service charges. For the coloreds, whites, and employed Africans, Cukutown was the unserviced, foul-smelling haven of gangsters, shebeen owners, street children, and prostitutes. The unfolding logic of urban development was to gradually bury it below the image of paved roads, grassed front lawns, clean shopping malls, laughing children walking safely to school, and all the other associations of urban modernity.

To give substance to this image, the urban elites who represented these constituencies had agreed to abide by municipal bylaws that outlawed shebeens in Phoenix and Slovo Park. Presumably they all suffered the illusion that heavy drinking in illegal shebeens was the cause of urban crime.

Sipho has just received a phone call from a white businessperson who plays a leading role in the Milnerton Ratepayers Association. The conversation went something like this:

"Sipho, how are you?"

"Fine, Harry." Sipho waits because these calls always have a purpose.

"Sipho, I was just sitting here thinking about how things are going with the project and I was wondering whether I should come and see you because it really has been quite some time since we sat down and had a good heart-to-heart chat." Sipho knew there was no truth that this call was because Harry was sitting around with nothing to do but to think about how nice it would be to have a chat. Harry was trying to appear informal and friendly when in fact Sipho knew he did nothing without a reason. What could it be this time, Sipho wondered?

"Yes, Harry, it has been too long. You know, guys around here have been asking me about you, wanting to know when you are going to come around again to see what is happening on the ground. We have a lot of problems here." Sipho smiled to himself; this is exactly what Harry does not want to hear about.

Quickly getting back to why he phoned, Harry continued, "How about later today, Sipho, can you make that?"

"No, unfortunately not, Harry. As you know we always have our residents' meeting on Tuesday nights and I must meet the executive members this afternoon to plan things. How about the end of the week? Things should be easier by then."

"No, it can't wait."

"Oh, is there a problem, Harry?" Sipho's delaying tactics had paid off—so there was a specific problem after all.

"Yes, I really must talk to you urgently. Are you sure you cannot make later today—I mean, do you personally have to go to the residents' meetings? Don't they happen every week? Surely missing one would not be so problematic. Surely you have someone to delegate these kinds of things to. I really have an important matter that must be attended to."

"Sorry, Harry, I have to be there. Can we not deal with this over the phone?"

"Well, okay. Look, Sipho, the ratepayers are getting very concerned about two things. I must add that I have also chatted to the chaps from Phoenix and they feel the same as us. In fact, we met all weekend with them to discuss the matter."

"What matter? What's bothering you?"

"We have information that as people move to Slovo Park they are not demolishing their shacks as promised. This means Cukutown is not getting smaller, which means it may always exist. And worst of all, the shebeens are not closing down, which means that all the bad elements and criminals continue to hang around in Cukutown. Are you aware of all this, Sipho?"

"Well, kind of. I have been trying to find out more," Sipho lied. He was fully aware of what was going on but at a loss as to what to do about it. Stall for time, he thought, that always gives me a breather to figure out what to do.

"Well, we have all the information you will need, Sipho. I think that we should meet with the police to work out a plan to make sure our agreements are adhered to. What do you think?"

"That's okay, but I think we should take it to the community first. I mean we agreed all along in this project that things must be done in a participatory way. I am sure the community will understand your problems and we can find out what is really happening."

"We know what is really happening; but okay, I can see that going straight to the police may cause a blow up. But let's agree that after the meeting we'll make a plan to bring in the police to deal with the matter. Okay?" Harry's voice was irritated now.

"Okay, but let's see what comes up at the meeting. How about the next monthly meeting of the forum—that is where all the reps sit. There is nowhere else to meet them."

"Yes, okay, I suppose that will have to do. Bye, Sipho."

Whew, that gives me 3 weeks, Sipho thought. I am sure Harry did not realize that the meeting is that far away. Sipho looked out the window of his prefab office where trucks were dumping topsoil for building the new roads for Slovo Park and he pondered about the consequences of what was really happening.

What the developers, residents, NGOs and local authorities had ignored at the outset was the fact that quite a number of relatively well-off people who moved from Cukutown to Slovo Park were owners of the shebeens in Cukutown and depended on revenue from the shebeens for survival when they lived in Cukutown. Now that they have moved to Slovo Park, they have continued to depend on this revenue to help pay for their service changes and bonds on their new residences. Furthermore, when the compact was signed, everyone ignored the possibility that some Cukutowners would not demolish their shacks behind them after moving to Slovo Park because either they intended to return after selling their Slovo Park units in order to realize their government subsidies as cash, or they intended renting out their shacks to newcomers in order to help with the bond repayments and service charges in Slovo Park.

Slovo Park–based shebeen owners are not allowed to open shebeens in Slovo Park. However, Sipho knew of quite a few who were still operating their shebeens in Cukutown. In order to make sure that the shebeens remain a viable source of revenue to subsidize the costs of living in Slovo Park, the shebeen owners have an interest in making sure that Cukutown does not disappear. The best way to achieve this would, of course, be to encourage others to keep their shacks to rent out to newcomers to the area and to assist the poorest of the poor to realize their government subsidies as raw cash by selling their Slovo Park units and moving back to Cukutown. In so doing, the shebeen owners will have effectively ensured the survival of Cukutown as a protected space where the poorest of the poor, the gangsters, prostitutes, street children, the wrecked, and increasingly the illegal aliens from neighboring countries can continue to survive anonymously and largely without paying for staying in the city. The result will be a pact between those whose survival depends on anonymity and those who profit from protecting the informal spaces that ensure anonymity.

Sipho was only too aware of the consequences of bringing in the police because once again the Cukutowners would rally against these outside threats, just as they did during apartheid. Sipho wondered if his old comrade Buli—from the street battles of those days—was still around. "I am sure he wouldn't think twice about fighting the police again," Sipho muttered to himself.

Breaking away from the memories of those bitter battles, Sipho brought himself back to the realities of the moment, realizing that it was up to him to provide leadership. He had three weeks until the meeting of the forum. He could ignore the matter and let everyone fight it out at the forum or he could drop all the other important work related to the development of Slovo Park in order to meet the shebeen owners to come up with a way of handling this. Would they cooperate and be straight with him? Maybe I can find Buli, again, he thought. Or should I bring in the NGOs and developers to come up with a job creation strategy so that the shebeen owners could find other sources of income? He also knew that Harry would contact as many other players about the problem just in case, Sipho thought to himself, I decide to do nothing about this mess—that's his style.

Mark Swilling is a professor at the University of Stellenbosch, South Africa, and a member of the Sustainability Institute of South Africa. This case is based on an unpublished research report that was commissioned as part of the Ford Foundation–funded Global Urban Research Initiative project. The reference to the report is as follows: Robbins, S., "'In the land of the blind, the one-eyed man is king': Development and Power Brokers in an Informal Settlement in Cape Town," March 1997. The conversations reported in the case are imagined rather than actual or true events and are based on projections about the type of relationships that are described by Robbins in his case.

8

Reporting the Local News

Terence J. Reidy

Victor was an experienced public manager who held the position of town manager in several communities over his 20-year career as a public servant. Prior to his career in government he had worked as a social worker and as a newspaper reporter. Currently he is the manager of Petersburg, a community known for its willingness and success at addressing social issues. It is a town whose residents are involved in the media, arts, and entertainment as well as major corporations and finance. It is a sophisticated community with a flair for social causes and attracting media coverage.

Along the way, his career was as much community organizer and social worker as it was anything else, so when Victor arrived in Petersburg, he felt very in tune with the social issues and understood the benefit of open communication with the residents. His last community was the county seat and received newspaper coverage from two daily newspapers and one local weekly. He was used to discussing the news of the day with at least two reporters and had a working relationship, which allowed him some flexibility in speaking off the record. All in all, Victor was considered an effective communicator and a professional at dealing with newspapers.

A couple of years into his tenure in Petersburg, and after some minor skirmishes with the local weekly newspaper, *The Petersburg Gazette*, Victor had established a good rapport with the editor and staff. There were still complaints from his department heads that notices were not published on time and that coverage of municipal events was spotty, but Victor felt that his relationship with the editor and his ability to tell the town's side of the most important stories overshadowed these complaints.

The editor of the *Gazette*, Maria, related to him on a deeper level than most people. She promoted the manager's initiatives and gave him high marks on his performance. Maria often remarked, "The more difficult the challenge the more enthusiastic Victor's response." He thrived on challenges addressing racial issues, sex discrimination, and affordable housing, as well as the challenges associated with fostering interlocal agreements designed to save taxpayers money and enhance service delivery.

Maria wrote several glowing editorials about Victor's achievements and the strides he had made in promoting racial harmony and the image of Petersburg as a great place to live and raise children.

It was about this time that Victor was contacted by a faculty member from the state university who was writing a grant application to a major foundation to fund a project that was designed to increase citizen participation in government by developing citizen-driven measures for town services.

Victor was fascinated by the idea. "This is a wonderful opportunity," he told the professor. "We could bring concerned residents into the conversation from the beginning as opposed to always reacting to their complaints and trying to convince them that their tax dollars are being used effectively."

The professor had already approached several larger municipalities, including the capital, but had been turned away. "I was hoping I could count on you," he replied. "The other municipalities were concerned that including the residents in an accountability system would be too much of a political risk."

"Well," Victor responded, "even though I'm excited about this opportunity there still may be some reluctance and political risk; we'll just have to take this one step at a time. The first step will be to introduce the concept to the governing body and the department heads and get their buy-in."

Victor was pleased that the *Petersburg Gazette* accurately and consistently followed the story, informing the public and giving the government credit for venturing into this area.

About 2 years into the project, Maria left the city for a rural community and a position teaching journalism at a small university.

When Maria left the paper, it was sold to a conglomerate that owned several city papers, and coverage of government affairs changed dramatically. Their priority was selling papers and advertising space, not honest reporting of local events. The new editor, Irynna, was determined to make a name for herself. At a meeting of the local chapter of the League of Women Voters, Irynna told the members of the audience that her job as editor of the local paper was to "generate controversy," and that she did. While Maria, the former editor, accurately reported policy initiatives and government issues of interest to her readers, Irynna failed to do so.

Understanding the importance of maintaining a good relationship with the paper, Victor invited Irynna to one of his staff meetings. The meeting went well, the new editor said all the right things and promised Victor and his directors that she would improve coverage of the town and pay attention to deadlines for town-sponsored events. Victor had a separate meeting with the editor to introduce her to the citizen-driven government performance project.

"I'm very proud to be part of this project," Victor explained to Irynna. "Our town has the benefit of three years' worth of research and education, all the resources of our state university, and the funding of a national foundation. I am optimistic that we will increase our residents' understanding of what we do and we will better understand the expectations of our citizens." Irynna nodded and smiled and made comments that gave Victor the impression that she understood the significance of the work and the risk that Victor was taking.

Six months later, however, not only had coverage of the town not improved, but it had gotten worse. Victor spoke to Irynna about the coverage and the cartoons depicting the town in a negative light; Irynna apologized and promised to use a more balanced approach. This was to be the beginning of a series of meetings, apologies, and promises to do better and then more of the same. Victor included Irynna's publisher, Katherine, in some of these meetings, but to no avail.

"Oh, Irynna is a real character," Katherine noted. "You should see her ranting and raving about town services around the editorial room."

Victor asked Katherine what could be done to address this behavior; she shrugged her shoulders.

Victor shared this experience with other local officials and found that Irynna had the same routine—civil to your face, uncivil in the press. Victor saw that Irynna's criticisms were escalating. He also noted that the criticisms were becoming more personal and directed at him.

Meanwhile, the foundation-funded project progressed. There were numerous meetings held throughout the town. Members of the town council were interviewed and their issues and concerns were documented for the project. Education sessions were held with municipal staff and citizens alike. Weeks turned into months and the work continued.

The task at hand was a daunting one: So many meetings and so much time had been invested. The governing body was split regarding the benefit of the project. The mayor was cautious and concerned that a handful of disgruntled residents would dominate the process, so he did not encourage his supporters to participate. One of the ward council members threatened to sabotage the process.

"I'll publicly attack this project if you don't make sure my name gets in the paper. This is an election year," the councilor screamed.

On the other hand, two of the council members were very supportive and worked diligently to bring more citizens into the dialogue. Councilor Jessie Von Ronck attended numerous citizen meetings, spoke out publicly encouraging residents to participate, and lobbied other council members to participate. Councilor Alex Kouts was also supportive. Councilor Kouts had a long history of service in the community and saw this as a wonderful tool to bring residents into the decision-making process.

During all of this, the newspaper gave the project little or no coverage. At this point, Victor decided that silence was better than negativity and decided not to advocate for additional coverage until the work was further along.

One of the key elements of the project was a townwide citizen satisfaction survey. This survey was intended to take the pulse of the community. Victor felt good about this. Since he had been in town, he had been looking for an unbiased assessment of town services. Finally, he would have one.

Victor was impressed, and so were the council members and department heads. Even those not in support of the project admitted that the citizens and the university did an excellent job developing the survey. The survey was mailed to more than 10,000 homes. The response was overwhelming. The next task was to calculate the results and share their findings with the community.

Before the results were even known to the university, the local newspaper ran a scathing editorial attacking the survey. Irynna entitled her editorial: "Rosy, Rosier, and Rosiest" and accused the university of skewing the survey; she claimed that the survey was biased and that it was designed to show Petersburg in a good light. Victor was stunned and outraged; the university staff could not believe that a newspaper would take such an uninformed position. "You have not spent enough time watching this editor," Victor told the university professors. "This editor makes it her business to place the town in a bad light. This, however, is a new low, even for her."

Councilor Van Ronck and Councilor Kouts, two representatives from the university, and Victor called the paper and set up a meeting with Irynna and her publisher Katherine to discuss the editorial. Victor felt good about this. He had met the publisher and she came across as a straight shooter. While Victor had little hope for the editor, he thought that the presence of two university professors and two elected officials would send a strong message to Katherine.

The meeting started well, the elected officials presented their support for this project and their desire to "set the record straight." They were very cordial and expressed great optimism about "clearing the air" and "establishing better lines of communication." The university professors laid out the elements of the survey and their scientific approach in great detail. They spent about 20 minutes walking everyone through the process; they gave examples of other surveys and the scientific checks and balances used to minimize bias.

All during the presentation, Irynna acted bored. She moved around in her seat looking at the ceiling. She rarely made eye contact and even yawned. This was making Victor angry. He knew that the university professors were sincere and acting professionally. Victor was close to calling Irynna on her unprofessional behavior, but thought better of it. He knew that the professors were experienced and hoped that they would make their case to the publisher and that she would call Irynna to task.

At the end of the presentation, Katherine smiled and thanked the professors. Irynna slowly turned their way and said: "Well, there is nothing that you have said that changes my mind."

Victor waited for Katherine to say something. She did not. Victor looked at the professors, encouraging them to respond. They did not. Victor felt the top of his head ready to explode. He knew the history of this woman. He knew that Irynna had been targeting the town and writing negative stories—looking for excuses to turn public sentiment against the public officials—especially Victor. He knew that if he took Irynna on in front of her boss that there would be hell to pay. And yet he could not let this poor excuse for an editor get away with undermining the work of this project. He knew that if the editorial went unchallenged residents might lose faith in the process. The early results were back and the majority of residents were satisfied with town services. Now the editorial would tarnish those findings.

Victor looked around the room. He knew that if he spoke, it would be direct and confrontational. He knew that he only had a moment before the meeting would be called to a close.

Terence J. Reidy is the city manager of Asbury Park, New Jersey.

9

Returning Home to Serve

Frederic Bogui

Actually it was a noble idea, considering that most foreign students living in Europe, after completion of their studies, often seek employment in Europe or elsewhere rather than return to their birth country to work. After obtaining his terminal degree in Paris, and against his friends' advice, Kouakou decided to return home to West Africa for a position in the public sector.

The decision was not an easy one. Kouakou was torn between his loyalty to his home country and his attraction to the comfortable life style that he had become accustomed to in Europe. The decision process was an agonizing one, coupled with the fact that the salary and benefits offered by his home government were not attractive. Kouakou knew that by accepting the job back home, he essentially was taking "a vow of poverty" as compared to a job in Europe. After days of anguish Kouakou accepted the position of director of social services in West Africa. He thought that he knew the challenges ahead.

On the return plane to home, he kept wondering if he was up to the challenges of his new position. Upon arrival, he was anxious to start, but it soon became apparent to him that he would be facing difficult choices in the scope of his employment. The most difficult part of his job was to figure out ways to satisfy the clients' increasing demand for services with diminishing resources. Indeed, when Kouakou took the job, he was warned by the preceding director that money was very scarce but citizen demands were in ample supply.

Kouakou soon found out the harsh reality of delivering services at the "street level." It is in these difficult moments of deciding whether to provide quality service or to conserve resources that Kouakou realized the true meaning of public administration and wondered whether the primary emphasis of his job should be on "public" demands or "administration" of resources.

Numerous requests to upper levels of management to increase his budget were rejected. In fact, the state budget was spread thin, and most departments were understaffed and undercapitalized. In spite of the difficult situation, Kouakou tried to make the best of it. But he did not feel welcomed and a part of the group. A colleague made the following remark to him:

"I know you did your graduate studies in Europe and you also worked for some years in Western countries where resources are available. While you were living a comfortable life in Europe, some of us stayed here and learned to work with the meager resources that we were given. So don't come in here and tell us what to do. We know our situation better than you do, and we don't like outsiders like you trying to show off."

"Outsider like him?" How could he say that? Kouakou sacrificed a lot to return home. Then he got to thinking. Maybe it was not just his colleagues who were unhappy with his return. His boss seemed to be acting uneasy around him sometimes, but he had thought he was just imagining it.

But he had made his choice, so he needed to make the best of it. Kouakou realized that he might need to probe money sources outside the organization to increase his budget. But increasingly, Kouakou felt that seeking outside grants to complement his budget would not be "the politically correct" thing to do. His boss might view this gesture negatively because Kouakou went beyond him to fix the problem. Moreover, Kouakou did not want to risk antagonizing upper management. After careful consideration, Kouakou postponed, at least for now, his plan to seek outside funding.

Another vexing problem that Kouakou faced was that most of his peers in other departments were reluctant to provide him with relevant work information. The root cause of this lack of information sharing among departments was the fact that files were either missing or not properly filed. This seemed to explain why there was no follow up on clients' requests and inquiries. Kouakou and his entire office staff were making decisions with incomplete information. This was a challenge that Kouakou felt that he could address.

But he also felt that he was risking the ire of the other department managers, who might feel that he was planning to expose the poor job they had been doing. In spite of the situation, Kouakou decided to remedy the problem by creating a central location for data accumulation and requested one of his staff to be in charge of the filing department. The ideal scenario would be to have clients' information on line for easy access, but Kouakou knew, because of budget constraints, that this would be an unrealistic request. For now, his central storage idea would improve information sharing among departments and help in providing better service to clients.

In spite of some limited success, Kouakou still feels uncomfortable. He knows that to really make a difference, he has to go after outside funding. He also knows that his colleagues will not take kindly to his attempts; they will think he is trying to show off, to illustrate to everyone that the other staffers are incompetent. He is lonely and frustrated. He wonders if he has made the right decision. He really wants to do the right thing, but if he isn't welcome at home, maybe he doesn't really belong here anymore.

Frederic Bogui, a native of the Ivory Coast, teaches public administration at Seton Hall University in South Orange, New Jersey.

10

Computer Problems at the Library

Ray Schwartz

The region's integrated library system is 10 years old and missing a variety of components, such as a reporting module. In order to use the present system to its fullest, the libraries would have to invest in additional software and training. Instead, they decided to purchase a new system from a leading competitor. Their intent is to acquire a system that will take advantage of the latest Web and Internet technologies and open standards. The regional government has given the libraries $300,000 for the purchase and installation of the new system.

The system is used in the management, procurement, and inventory of the libraries' collections of books, journals, microforms, and other research materials. Presently the libraries' system contains 250,000 records representing the materials they own and 13,000 records of their clients and transactional data. In order to install the new system, several major steps must be planned and coordinated: (a) These data must be converted from the old system to the new system with a minimal disruption of services, (b) the new system cannot be installed "out of the box" but must be configured for the local environment, and (c) since all staff use the old system as the main tool for their work, they must be thoroughly trained to use the new system.

The libraries are composed of a main library staffed with 3 managers, 7 professionals, and 12 support staff and a branch library staffed with a director and one professional. The three managers include the director, the assistant director, and the director of projects and grants. The director is ultimately responsible for the libraries and has three managers, eight professionals, and an administrative assistant reporting directly to him. The assistant director is responsible for the circulation department, integrated library system maintenance, and the acquisitions department, which handles all research material procurement except for journals. Her responsibilities include supervision of eight support staff. The director for projects and grants is responsible for the interlibrary lending and journals departments and four support staff. She works closely with one professional to assist her in these two departments, and she backs up the assistant director as needed. Four professionals work with library clients and local businesses.

The director has assigned the selection process, contract negotiation, training, implementation, and contract management to the assistant director. The assistant director organized an implementation committee composed of the director of the branch library, two professionals, and three support staff.

The regional executive signed the contract with the software vendor in February. Soon after, the libraries purchased the machines, and the assistant director established an implementation schedule beginning in March through the anticipated completion in September.

The assistant director resigned in late March, before the product installation and data conversion began. This resignation left the director in a difficult situation. Not only was the assistant director responsible for the implementation, but she was also responsible for three departments, support staff supervision, and evaluations. The library, by contract, is now committed to completing the implementation and they want to have it up and working by fall, when the children go back to school. No one at the library has the experience or the expertise to see this implementation through, and there is a hiring freeze in effect. All current positions in the libraries are assigned to handle ongoing operations. What is needed is someone who understands the workings of an integrated library system and the intricacies of the libraries' data. What should the director do?

Ray Schwartz is a librarian with the New Jersey Institute of Technology.

11

Getting Support for Good Works

Janna Ataiants

It was long believed that the former Soviet Union had managed to avoid a large-scale AIDS epidemic. According to the United Nations' reports, however, HIV transmission in the former Soviet Union is growing with the fastest rate in the world. In a 6-year period, the number of HIV-positive cases has risen from just 30,000 to nearly 1 million. Responding to the epidemic, the former Soviet Union established a network of government AIDS centers at both the regional and local levels to provide the population with information and preventive services.

International humanitarian aid to cope with the AIDS epidemic in the former Soviet Union is growing each year. The United Nations' agencies and international nongovernmental organizations (NGOs) have been actively involved in the fight against the disease and have become the main sponsors of local NGOs dealing with HIV/AIDS.

Medicines to People is an international humanitarian organization, based in the United States, that helps developing countries cope with serious infectious diseases, including HIV/AIDS. When a major international donor approached Medicines to People and invited them to submit a proposal to conduct HIV training seminars for health care providers in the former Soviet Union, the organization felt the project would be a right thing to do, even though training was not their area of expertise. Medicines to People is a well-respected organization, and the funders felt confident their money would be well spent. Medicines to People also knew the money was theirs for the asking: It was an invitation too good to turn down.

Medicines to People, as expected, received the funding. The grant was awarded for one year to prepare and conduct four identical 5-day training seminars in four locations in the former Soviet Union. The training seminars themselves were scheduled to be conducted 3 months prior to the end of the contract year. Such a schedule allowed sufficient time for preparation and was convenient for the seminar trainers.

Soon after receiving the grant, however, the organization had to make several changes to the initial proposal. First of all, Medicines to People learned that as time went by, only one of the four preselected sites—an AIDS center in the city of Belogorsk—remained positive toward the collaboration, and the other sites had other priorities and interests. Thus, it was decided to conduct just one training seminar—in Belogorsk. However, to satisfy the donor and provide training to health professionals from four regions, all four sites were invited to send several participants to the seminar in Belogorsk.

In addition, one of the trainers who had experience in the former Soviet Union advised the organization to compress the 5 days of training into 2 days of training because it would be difficult for local people to take a week off from work.

Three months prior to the proposed training, Medicines to People received verbal permission from the donor to conduct one 2-day seminar in Belogorsk. The organization, however, still had to finalize many logistical issues with their local partners. Even more worrisome was the difficulty in establishing working contacts with two powerful AIDS players in the Republic—the local UN representatives and the Republican AIDS Center. Medicines to People wrote them letters and sent faxes and e-mails—but they received no response.

Two months prior to the training seminar, Melanie Geans, Medicines to People's program manager responsible for this project, was sent for a site visit to Belogorsk to finalize the logistics of the training. In Moscow Melanie was joined by Volodya Korolev, who translated for Medicines to People whenever the organization conducted projects in the former Soviet Union, as Russian was still the language of choice in many former Soviet Republics.

Unexpectedly, thanks to Irina, a local contact who was found via a partner international NGO, Melanie and Volodya received an invitation to attend a meeting with local representatives of the UN in the capital of the republic.

The meeting participants included two UN officials, both natives of the former Soviet Union, and the director of the Republican AIDS Center.

From the beginning of the meeting Melanie felt hostility in the air. The conversation was led by Dr. Georgy Apaguni, the director of the Republican AIDS Center. After an initial pause, Apaguni coldly inquired, "Please tell us about your organization and your project."

Volodya tried to translate this conversation with as much diplomacy as he could master, but Melanie had no difficulty understanding the tone. "They are against our training before they know anything about us," she thought. She briefly explained project goals and the scope of proposed activities.

"When do you intend to conduct your training?"

"In 2 months."

"In 2 months? This is impossible! Are you aware that in two months the Republican AIDS Center, with the cooperation of the United Nations, is hosting a National Conference on HIV/AIDS treatment protocol? You *should* postpone your seminar until after the National Conference takes place."

"But we already set our plans for the training and our local partners in Belogorsk expect us to hold the seminar in 2 months . . ."

"We did not know anything about your plans until this very minute, and it looks like your organization is not interested in HIV-related human-itarian activity here. Are you aware of the role of the Republican AIDS Center regarding the AIDS epidemic in the region? Why you did not come here first and seek our advice regarding your project?"

Melanie wanted to say, "Apaguni may think he can control the HIV agenda here, but we do not have to report to him about our project," but she decided to stay as polite as possible. And what good would it do to use the same hostile tactics of allegations and confrontation at this meeting? If the Republican AIDS Center decided not to cooperate with Medicines to People, it would simply mean the end of the training project. Their policy was to work collaboratively with local officials, not conduct a project if it was against the will of the established organizations working in the Republic.

"Dr. Apaguni, we have a great respect for the Republican AIDS Center and its activities in the region. We tried to contact the center several times to arrange a meeting, unfortunately with no success. Both electronic and phone communications between the United States and the Republic are very difficult." Of course, Melanie did not add that, in her opinion, the Republican AIDS Center simply ignored her inquiries.

Maybe the words "great respect" had some soothing effect on Apaguni as he continued in a less aggressive manner:

"Actually, holding off this training can benefit your organization more than you may now know. Don't you realize that in order to be sustainable, your training should be conducted in accordance to the national AIDS treatment protocol?"

"We do realize that. It's just that the news about the National Conference was so sudden. I think we will definitely reschedule our training." Melanie thought, "We must convince our donor, trainers, and local partners about the need to postpone the project, and hopefully everybody's schedule will fit into the new dates . . ."

The conversation was getting friendlier, and at the end the UN officials even invited representatives from Medicines to People to attend the upcoming National Conference.

After the meeting, Melanie was interested in Volodya's impression of the meeting.

"I think it was surprisingly fruitful," he said. "To be honest, I had no hope in the beginning, but it turned out to be fruitful."

"Do you think their invitation to attend the National Conference is sincere?"

Volodya hesitated a bit. "My opinion, and it is just my personal opinion, is that they invited us because we came here out of respect for their efforts. I think they might actually be relieved if we kept in touch, followed up, but did not actually attend the conference."

The next day, Melanie and Volodya went to Belogorsk, where they were warmly received by the local team. Unfortunately, Melanie's story about her encounter with Dr. Apaguni caused strong resentment among the local partners.

"They are just a bunch of bureaucrats acting all important in the capital," they said. "Asking us to postpone our training until the National Conference is simply a stalling tactic; a bureaucratic procedure. It will not change anything."

"Well, we should be diplomatic and adhere to the wishes of those bureaucrats," Melanie said.

"Unfortunately, this is our reality," the chief doctor said. "Actually, I think your organization made a mistake when asking Irina, your local contact, to set up a meeting with the local UN representatives and Dr. Apaguni. Apparently, she was not the best person to set you up. . . . To be honest, I would not trust her to communicate with those people on behalf of your organization in the future. You should understand that everything here in the former Soviet Union is made via informal networks, and you have to be very careful in choosing your 'intermediaries.'"

As a result, the training seminar was rescheduled after the National Conference and only 1 month prior to the end of their funding contract. A lot of logistical work had to be done yet; however, unexpectedly Melanie got a sense of relief regarding this project. "At least we know nothing else can go wrong," Melanie thought. "Everything that could change has changed—the number of places, the seminar length, and the seminar dates."

She was mistaken. Three weeks before the Medicines to People seminar, Melanie received an e-mail from Irina, who informed her that the National Conference was unexpectedly rescheduled and would be held 10 days after the end of Medicines to People's grant. Melanie was devastated. To postpone the seminar again would mean losing credibility with the donor and possibly the loss of funds. At the same time, the last thing Melanie wanted was another confrontation with Dr. Apaguni and the Republican AIDS Center.

Melanie picked up a phone and dialed the executive director's extension. "We need to meet, and it's urgent . . ."

Janna Ataiants was program coordinator for the Moscow Office of the Eurasia Foundation and currently is enrolled in the public administration program at Rutgers University–Campus at Newark.

12

An Office Romance

RaJade Berry

As a recent college graduate, Mary accepted the position of administrative assistant in one of the largest public universities in the region. She had secured a fantastic position where career development and personal growth would be inevitable. Her supervisor, Bill, was a faculty member from the public administration department and was very enthusiastic about her engagement in the public sector. From the start, he was eager to have Mary accompany him on conferences around the country. In just a short period of time, Mary had been to 12 conferences in Asia, Africa, Europe, and the United States. She was having the time of her life.

During the same month that Mary started working, two of her soon-to-be best friends joined the institution as well. Each of the women was about the same age—in their early 20s—and eager to learn as much as they could about the institution and the career opportunities that awaited them. At the college, Claudette, a native of Jamaica, worked as a secretary, and Juanita, a recent college graduate, worked as an advisor to student groups. From the very beginning, the three women got along very well and formed an immediate bond that would stand the test of time.

On occasion, Claudette and Mary would go out to lunch with Mary's supervisor, Bill. When the three of them had lunch last, Claudette, Mary, and Bill went to a local Indian restaurant. During lunch, Claudette sat next to Mary and directly across from Bill. Mary was babbling about the next board of trustees meeting when all of a sudden Bill seemed to jump right off of his seat. At first, she was startled and wondered if he was choking on one of the Indian delicacies. When she turned to look at her friend, Claudette had a guilty look on her face. Unaware of what was happening,

Mary continued the conversation and planned to speak about the incident with Claudette later.

After they got back from lunch, Mary called Claudette and asked her to meet in one of the ladies' lounges. As soon as she walked into the bathroom, Mary asked her what went on during lunch. She responded, "Bill and I were playing footsies under the table. He is such a great guy. For a long time, I've been wanting to tell you that I think he's in love with me." Mary was shocked. Her supervisor was more than 25 years their senior and had a beautiful wife. He was more than just a "boss" to Mary. In fact, in the short time that she worked with him, he had always been an honorable man: giving her career advice, encouraging her to pursue an advanced degree, and acting much like a father figure. Deep in her heart, Mary knew Claudette had misinterpreted Bill's generosity and confused his concern for romantic affection. For the rest of the summer, she decided against going to lunch with Claudette and Bill.

After several years, Juanita and Mary sought new managerial positions at the institution. Juanita was the first to interview for the position of affirmative action officer at the university. While some at the university believed Juanita didn't have enough experience in affirmative action, she had obtained a certificate in affirmative action and received her MBA in human resources. After a lengthy application process, Juanita was offered the job. In the meantime, Mary was preparing for a career move in academic affairs within the university. She accepted a new position in academic advisement and worked with student majors in several departments throughout the university.

More than 6 years had passed since Mary worked with Bill. There were quite a number of changes that were taking place at the college. As fate would have it, Bill was appointed as the interim president. However, there were several factions on the campus that opposed his presidential candidacy. Early in the academic year in which Bill was serving as interim president, some had even gone so far as to suggest that Bill wasn't suitable to assume the role of president because he had sexually harassed Mary's friend Claudette.

Although Mary had heard of the rumors alleging sexual harassment, she was certain that Claudette hadn't started them. After some investigation of her own, Mary found out that Thomas, a midlevel manager at the university who opposed Bill's presidency, felt compelled to bring the accusation to the attention of the senior administration. Since Juanita was the affirmative action officer, she was asked to investigate Thomas's claim that Bill sexually harassed Claudette more than 10 years earlier. During his interview, Thomas also told Juanita that Mary was aware of the details of the harassment and could provide enough factual information to substantiate the claim. Juanita began an official investigation. The first person interviewed was Claudette. After discussing with Claudette the policy on sexual harassment, Juanita asked Claudette if Bill had sexually harassed her in any way. Claudette said, "No, he would never do that. Bill and I are just friends." Juanita prepared a written report for the board of trustees indicating that she found no evidence that sexual harassment had occurred.

Despite the political maneuvers on campus, Bill quickly appointed his presidential team and began to work on his agenda for the institution. Mary was asked to serve as a special assistant to the president to work on specific institutional assignments, although she still maintained her position in academic affairs. For the most part, many of Bill's colleagues celebrated his appointment and his candidacy for president. Yet there were still some who resented his appointment and sought to make sure that he would not be selected as the next president of the university.

About 6 months into Bill's presidency, Mary was contacted by the attorney general's office. Since she was unsure of the nature of the call, Mary called Juanita right away. Juanita indicated that they shouldn't talk about the situation over the telephone so they arranged to meet at a discreet location on campus. Juanita said, "I just learned that someone contacted the attorney general's office to have Bill investigated for sexual harassment."

Mary asked, "How could they do that when you've already investigated that allegation?"

Juanita said, "I've been removed as the affirmative action officer regarding this case because someone suggested that I let our friendship affect my findings in the case."

Mary was dumbfounded and couldn't believe what she was hearing. She said, "What in the hell is going on here? I called Claudette before I came over and was told that she was on an administrative leave of absence. When I called her at home, her husband said that she moved to Georgia to live with her sister for a while." Although the recent events were alarming, some of the pieces were starting to fall together. As Juanita and Mary figured, Claudette left town because she was afraid of an investigation by the attorney general's office. From what they could tell, a friend of Claudette's had come forward and said that Claudette told her that Bill had sexually harassed her in the past. Whoever asked the attorney general's office to investigate the claim knew that Claudette told someone directly she was sexually harassed.

Mary was unsure of her next steps. Deep in her heart, she felt that this investigation was just like the previous one. She thought it was a political maneuver to have Bill eliminated as a presidential candidate. From talking with others on campus, she knew that the president of the largest public university in the region carried a great deal of political weight. As a result, whoever was selected as president stood to influence public policy regarding future higher-education initiatives. In reality, Mary was scared. She worked hard to establish a career in higher education and felt that if she participated in the investigation in any way, her participation could come back to haunt her. Mary thought her career options in higher education and in the public sector could be harmed if the investigation was made public.

The representatives from the attorney general's office had been on campus the previous day and had spoken to several people who were close to Mary. From what her colleagues told her, Mary was as much a part of the investigation as she was the key witness. The representatives asked about her personal character, her close relationship with Bill, and her motives for success. Before she agreed to cooperate with the investigation, Mary called a lawyer friend for advice. She wasn't sure what she should do.

RaJade Berry teaches public administration at the University of Akron, Ohio.

13

Moving Up in the Organization

Belinda Van Wyk

Nick Brown is 49 years old and employed as a director in the Stores and Provisions Department. He joined the section 31 years ago as a clerk and worked his way up the ladder. Although his advancement has been slow, he believed that it was well deserved. He regarded this as his final position, as the chief director was only 1 year older than he was.

The problem on Nick's desk now is what to do with Mike. Mike, his deputy director, had come to talk to him about resigning, and this would create serious problems for the section. Nick clearly remembered the day, albeit 14 years ago, when Mike presented himself for an interview. He was only 18 years old, energetic, and full of bright ideas. At the interview he stated that he would study and try his best.

Mike joined the Stores and Provisions Department as a junior clerk, but he continued his studies. He matured quickly and successfully integrated much of his classroom work into useful projects at the office. Mike was by far the most dedicated and motivated employee. Coupled with his good academic abilities and the skill he possessed to mix theory with practice in the real world, he soon advanced to the position of chief clerk.

Mike continued to study and was promoted to the position of administration officer. At the office he worked even harder streamlining the administrative processes. These measures were seen as being very useful and functional. The following year he conducted an internal audit in which unnecessary duplication was identified and eradicated. His efforts were applauded and he was once again promoted, this time to the position of senior administrative officer.

Mike then enrolled in a graduate degree program in public management. During the same year he revised and analyzed the existing departmental policies, a move that earned him the admiration of all his superiors. At the end of that year he took the position of assistant director. Mike was then only 29 years old. The following year he completed his MPA (master's in public administration) and was promoted to the position of deputy director, a position that he has held ever since.

After a year, he was given a merit increment, which placed him on the top of his salary scale. Mike continued to propose changes but was increasingly experiencing more resistance from the chief director. On numerous occasions, Nick tried to support Mike, but with little success. Nick was being squashed in the middle of these differences and found the predicament rather exhausting. Mike's most recent project involved an organizational restructuring exercise and the development of a staff appraisal system. Nick thought that the proposal deserved consideration, but the chief director disagreed and hired an external consultant to complete the same task. Mike was frustrated.

Mike was now only 32 years old, and the promise of further advancement was almost certain. He would, however, have to wait for almost 15 years! As he met with more and more resistance, Mike became more and more unmotivated. The chief director saw Mike's lack of motivation as a sure result of immaturity and the inability to handle minor setbacks.

Nick suspected a problem but lacked the energy to address it until Mike came to his office to say that he had been offered a teaching position at a technical training school. Nick really did not want to see Mike leave— he was such a star performer—and he suspected that Mike didn't really want to leave either. But what can he do?

Belinda Van Wyk is a member of the faculty at the University of Stellenbosch, South Africa.

14

Training Grant Decisions

Richard Blake and Paulette Laubsch

Jim Corliss is the administrator of a government agency that has responsibility for sanctioning, funding, and monitoring training grants to public, private, and not-for-profit organizations. Due to a significant loss of manufacturing jobs, once the mainstay of the region's economy, government decided to create and dedicate revenues to a new program: the Workforce Development Partnership Program (WDPP). Jim is the administrator of this program. WDPP has two functions: (a) Pay for retraining eligible displaced workers and (b) pay eligible employing organizations for their own training purposes.

Employing organizations—public, private, and not-for-profit—typically have a wide range of needs for training. These organizations can design their own grants in a way that is suitable to their own unique purposes: a process known as customized training. Typically, training grants are for legal, management, and technical matters. Funding for International Standards Organization (ISO) certification is one element of customized training.

The ISO is a global, voluntary organization whose members are leaders from business, government, industry, and the professions. Operating without a legal mandate, it holds de facto authority in matters pertaining to quality and international trade. Certification by ISO is a tangible signal of quality to a broad range of clients, customers, regulators, and suppliers.

ISO certification is expensive. Organizations must be evaluated, trained to standardized procedures, implement these procedures, and be monitored throughout the process. ISO, through its national and local affiliates, has people who are experts in its procedures. These experts may be employed in the businesses that are certified or seeking certification or they may be contractually retained as consultants.

Jim's program has the authority and ability to award grants to organizations to pay for ISO certification as one element of customized training. These grants may cover assessment of current operations and extend through training and monitoring to the actual certification. Eligible organizations may use the funding to pay salaried employees, to hire outside consultants, or any such combination.

The WDPP is not an entitlement. Eligibility for a grant depends upon assessment of an organization's proposal and available WDPP revenues. Although the funding is dedicated as a percentage of a specified tax, the actual proceeds from the tax can fluctuate, depending on the economy. Consequently, it is difficult to plan from year to year, and grant decisions are typically tentative until the actual revenues are secured. During its first four years of operations, requests for the ISO certification component of customized training increased exponentially. It now dominates the grants.

Data indicate that large companies predominate the grants, with requests for ISO certification training the norm. Medium and small businesses are underrepresented in customized training, and this is especially true of female- and minority-owned businesses. Jim suspects that the requirement to match the grant may be a big problem for those smaller companies. He is even more upset by the fact that he feels that he is administering a program that provides support to rich companies at the expense of the smaller companies, and this isn't what he or the legislature had in mind when the program began.

As time goes on, however, more and more large organizations are seeking grants for customized training to assist in getting ISO certification. Small and medium firms, as well as not-for-profit agencies, are getting a smaller and smaller share of the pie. And the available funds are diminishing. To make matters worse, one very large company and recipient of one of the larger ISO training grants has announced their decision to move their operation out of the region to an area where operating costs would be less. Jim feels that this is a betrayal: The WDPP invested large sums to elevate the status of this company and the company pays them back by leaving town.

Jim's immediate task is to prepare for a meeting in a week with elected officials, in which he has to report, orally and in writing, past activities and future plans. Although he has statistics that would indicate that the WDPP is thriving, he is not at all happy with who is being served.

Richard Blake teaches in the social work program at Seton Hall University in South Orange, New Jersey.

Paulette Laubsch teaches in the School of Administrative Sciences, Fairleigh Dickinson University, Teaneck, New Jersey.

15

Getting the Staff On Board

Kamal Chavda

Nicholas Guerin was appointed city manager of Moyenne 2 months ago. During his interview and subsequent discussions with city council members, he was told that Moyenne needed someone who could market the city more aggressively to businesses. The major areas of concern outlined by the council members included new ecological initiatives to alleviate pollution, more affordable housing, conservation of natural areas, job training, transportation alternatives to ease the city's congestion problem, and improving neighborhood vitality, particularly in reference to the crime-ridden inner city.

Now that he's familiar with the day-to-day operations of his office and has established good rapport with most of the city's agency heads, Nicholas decides it is time to look into some of the challenges he has been hired to address. He sends out an e-mail listing of the major areas of concern to Jane Hernandez, director of the Community Development Department. Nicholas specifically requests that she solicit input from her managers and come up with a report listing in some detail the advantages and disadvantages associated with each proposal.

The following week, Nicholas receives the report, but to his amazement, it only contains ideas he has already heard from the department head informally when he first came to Moyenne. To get a better understanding of what is happening, he asks Jane to call a meeting with all of the managers in her department.

A week later Nicholas, Jane, and her eight managers find themselves in the conference room of the Community Development Department. Nicholas starts the meeting by talking about the problems faced by the inner city and asking people how they would revitalize the area. The eight managers look at Jane and exchange glances with one another, but no one utters a word. Nicholas looks at Jane, who then says, "Well, Nicholas, as I mentioned to you in my report, I think one of the first things we need to address is the old shopping center. The structure itself is dilapidated, most of the businesses have closed their doors, and it has become a popular spot for gang members to deal drugs. We ought to demolish the entire complex and build a housing development with one-bedroom apartments for low-income residents, with retail space on the first floor for resident-owned and -operated businesses . . ."

But Nicholas has stopped listening already. He's heard this spiel before. When Jane stops, the other managers in the room nod their heads in approval and turn toward Nicholas. They're waiting for his comments. Realizing this, Nicholas simply asks, "Any more suggestions?" But once again, the room falls silent. Nicholas begins to wonder if the managers even participated in the development of this proposal. "What directions did Jane give to her managers when I sent her the initial message? Did she seek any creative input from them? Did they do any brainstorming?" he asks himself. Once again, Jane breaks the silence, turns to her assistant director for housing and asks him to summarize the feasibility study he has started on the housing complex. The presentation that follows is thorough and professional, but Nicholas is thinking about something else.

It's clear to him that the proposal he's listening to is Jane's idea. She seems to have delegated to her managers the task of developing it and adding details. He recalls the atmosphere of the meetings he used to preside over when he was in charge of the Economic Development Department at Monplaisir. He remembers acting like a referee in a boxing match with a ring full of people. He didn't have to look at the people around the table in turns and wait for their ideas. No, he remembers people throwing out ideas, people interrupting one another; some would get off their chairs to be heard; others would be quick to raise criticisms. Yet this high level of interpersonal confrontation and argumentativeness was a testament to the energy, intensity, and enthusiasm found in the department. Individual creativity was highly regarded. This was reflected in the way decisions were reached: by conflict, compromise, and consensus, not by Nicholas alone. Nicholas also remembers being frustrated on occasion by the sheer number of brainstorming sessions he found himself in. He hardly remembers a time when he sat behind his desk, door shut, working on previously scheduled tasks without being interrupted. But he reminds himself that Monplaisir was listed among the top 10 most livable cities in the country 5 years in a row. He also has fond memories of the three best-practices awards his department received during his short tenure. In fact, he's certain that those honors are what got him his present city manager job.

The presentation is over. Nicholas thanks Jane and her staff. As they say good bye, Nicholas realizes that they all address Jane as Mrs. Hernandez. She uses their last names as well. Outside of the conference room, the atmosphere in the office is quiet; everyone sits in an office, with the doors closed. Those who are in the corridor go about their business quietly. Back in Monplaisir, the office had an open structure. People used to talk to one another over their computer monitors. Everyone was rushing from one end of the hall to the other. The atmosphere was definitely livelier and more informal. Even the dress code was casual.

Back in his office, Nicholas realizes he faces an unexpected internal problem: There is too much emphasis on rank and status within the Community Development Department. People are reluctant to offer unsolicited ideas for fear of disrespecting their senior colleagues or questioning their judgment. No one seems to act on his or her own initiative. Instead, they are content to wait for directives from above. There seems to be no lateral flow of communication. This is not the sort of environment that is conducive to innovative thinking and creativity. Nicholas knows that the quality of his work in Moyenne will depend on the creativity and innovativeness of his staff. The council is expecting a report within the month. Nicholas has his work cut out for him.

Kamal Chavda worked for the United Nations High Commissioner for Refugees in Nairobi, Kenya, and is an instructor at East Carolina University in Greenville, North Carolina.

16

Starting the New Job

Jessica de Koninck

Today is Linda's first day on her new job. Linda had been at her old job for almost seven years and liked it a lot. The work was challenging. She was well respected by her peers and had made some good friends. If not for a fabulous professional opportunity, she would be there still. In fact, if this job does not pan out, or when it ends, she would consider returning. Of course, the adage says, "You can't go home again," and she knows that to be true. But this is an opportunity too good to let pass by. A new state administration has entered office, and she is to be a key player in a department in an area where she has worked professionally for the past 20 years. Finally, she will have the opportunity to make things work the way she knows they can and should, and the people who are being brought on board with her share her concerns and interests. For the first time ever, Linda even had time to take a vacation after she ended her old job and before she started the new one. Her old boss even said, "If they're not good to you there, you come right back. We'll always have a place for you."

Her good luck may have ended there, though. Linda's husband became seriously ill while they were on vacation. They cut their trip short and expect extensive medical care. "Don't worry about me, honey," he says, but she is worried. Her new department has been waiting for several months for Linda to come on board. She thinks, "How will my new director feel about this? What about the transfer of my health benefits? The new plan is good. Will there be a problem?" Linda knows from years of experience how slow and bureaucratic government can be. This job is no exception. Ted, the human resources director, seems nice enough, but at her new employee orientation, when she explains her situation, Ted says, "Well, I just do not know how quickly we can move your paperwork through," and he avoids making eye contact. In the meantime, Linda is distracted. She answers brusquely, "You must get this done immediately." She is afraid her distractedness will lead to mistakes on the job.

Linda knows this job is not going to be easy. In addition to the complicated nature of the work, rumors abound. The department is dispirited. Many of the most knowledgeable employees took advantage of an early retirement program. This resulted in a painless, no layoffs, departmental downsizing. But they took their institutional memory with them, and some areas of the agency have no experienced staff. Most of the staff has civil service protection and many years of service. There are procedures for everything. Only a few managers, like her, are at-will employees. The department has the reputation of being filled with "go along—get alongs." Their unspoken motto is "I was here before you, and I will be here after you are gone."

The position she is filling is a particularly sensitive one, and the person serving in it changes with each administration. The last administration was in office for 8 years. After such a long time, all the changes of this new administration seem to be creating major turmoil. The department staff has become comfortable. Any change, even good change, always generates some discomfort. At Linda's interview her director asked a series of pointed questions directed to management style and signaling staff problems, questions like, "How are your people skills?" "What would you do about a difficult employee?" "What would you do if the people who work for you have difficulty working together, or cannot resolve any problems without bringing them to you?"

The department is housed in a large modern glass building in an office complex that looks as if it could be located anywhere in the world. In fact, the exterior physical location is one of the most attractive things about the place, but the building does not take advantage of that. Most people have no exterior view. The good news is that there is plenty of parking. The bad news is that the building is too far from the other government offices to be able to walk to them. This means her coworkers do not get out much and do not have personal relationships with the other agencies of government with whom they must work. Inside the building, there is no conference room large enough to accommodate either the entire staff or an entire floor of the staff. Sharing information will be a challenge. The interior space is arranged hierarchically. Linda's boss and one or two others have closed offices with windows. Another small group, including Linda, has windowless offices around an inner core. Everyone else works in a cubicle. Professional staff have cubicles with higher walls than the clerical staff. Since the floor plan is open, Linda knows it is going to take her days to find her way around. Most of her staff sit directly outside her door. She calls it "working in the hall."

Though not a morning person, Linda arrives early the first day. Her boss is already at work. "Good morning," she says and shows Linda to her office. She does not stop to talk with Linda or even share any expectations. Linda decides to wait until later in the day to share her personal concerns and to find out about immediate assignments. Linda's staff is eager to welcome her. They have provided donuts and coffee. She thinks things may work out well. But not just yet.

The department has just been reorganized. The chain of command has shifted, and not everyone is excited about where they have landed. Before Linda arrived, one of the secretaries in the section was assigned elsewhere. The position is vacant. Linda's not sure if filling it will be a struggle or if it will need to be filled at all. In the meantime, the secretary who left took all "her" office supplies with her. The secretary who remained exercised "self-help" the evening before and brought back "her" typewriter. One of the professional staff is on vacation. Another has already said, "I would like to be more involved in going to the regional meetings." Of course, her area does not cover regional meetings. So this does not appear a likely option for her. In the meantime, Linda's boss had locked the door of her office to keep her staff from moving things around.

Everyone is on best behavior this morning. Linda gets a little nervous when one of the secretaries explains that she will need to "know who's been doing what and who is not fulfilling their job responsibilities." Another staff member begins to mention a coworker's "attendance problems."

In the meantime, the change in administration means there are no existing procedures in Linda's area, even for day-to-day things. Her area is a politically sensitive one, and the outgoing staff was not eager to be replaced or to share their experience. It looks like she is going to have to be inventing a lot from scratch and that someone's feathers are sure to be ruffled. At the end of the day, Linda's boss stops by. She hands her a few papers and says very little other than, "This is a priority. You'll need to get on it right away." One project involves significant reallocation of funding priorities within the entire department. Lots of data will need to be collected, a lot of history retrieved, and a lot will need to be written and analyzed—all in a very short period of time or the opportunity will be lost. If the job is done well, the department may be able to function much more productively and much less expensively. It is still too early for Linda to assess how much work her staff can take on, what she will have to do herself, and who can be trusted. Her inclination is to roll up her sleeves and do everything herself until she can better assess her staff, but she knows that will really get things off to a terrible start. She also knows that her technical skills are her weakest area, but an area where her staff should be strong. She is best at applying the theory to the data. She wonders whether given her family pressures and the pressure of a new job she will be able to function effectively. Where does she go from here?

Jessica de Koninck is an attorney with the New Jersey Department of Education.

17

Friendships and the Job

Myung Jean Chun

Like on most mornings, Ming and Gurav had survived rush hour by listening to the news on Public Radio International. Ever since Gurav had gotten Ming his first job out of college they had been carpooling in Gurav's car. They were college best friends, had been roommates for years, and were now both software engineers at a small company, Caliber Technologies, that was a contractor of the National Economic Development Agency (NEDA).

When Ming got to the office he settled down at his terminal, logging onto Yahoo Messenger—the unofficial office intranet. This was how he started every day. Along with the usual work-related questions, there was an e-mail notifying him of an all-hands-must-attend meeting.

"What's up with the meeting?" popped up an IM (instant message) from Tyler. Tyler had the cube next to Gurav and had also been introduced to Caliber Technologies through Gurav. For about 3 years the three of them, along with their manager Ivan, had been the core development team. They had developed most of the product in a cramped room filled with friendly banter and a willingness to help with each other's work.

"Uhh, dunno . . . probably nothing important," typed Ming.

"I don't like it," typed Tyler. Then before Ming could respond, up popped the IM message, "What's Gurav doing?"

As Ming looked around the office, he noticed Gurav packing his belongings in a box.

"Gurav's packing. Not good," Ming typed.

But before Ming could get to Gurav, Sheldon, the founder and one of the managers, rounded the corner. "Group meeting—get to the meeting."

At the meeting the CEO started by outlining the company's financial situation: "Now everyone knows that we missed our fourth quarter numbers, and NEDA is on our back for a definite delivery date."

He then filled everyone in on the previous night's emergency board of directors meeting. The company was going to retool and refocus. And then the fateful words "and so we need to cut back." With a looming cash flow problem the company needed to do more with less. Since the product was nearly complete, everyone who was not essential was let go, five from development and one from sales.

People around the table began to count heads to see who was missing. Gurav was gone, as were some others. Ming didn't know what to say. His friend had been with the company longer than the majority of the people at the meeting, including the CEO. Resentment built and he looked at the people responsible for the mistakes that had cost them time and clients. Gurav had been one of the first hires and one of the most creative developers, and yet people who had been at the company a shorter time and had done less work were staying on. Ming didn't trust the CEO, but without more information he found himself unable to speak his mind. He also realized that it might be a bad move politically. It occurred to him that this was the first time he had thought about office politics.

He mulled over those who had been cut and why. Gurav had always done exemplary work as far as Ming could tell. Ming was very sure that Gurav had never been given a heads up that his work was not up to par. The company didn't have formal performance reviews, but still there wasn't any warning that this was going to happen.

But thinking back, there had been an inkling of trouble when Gurav and Tyler complained about their new manager. When the company expanded, the core development team had been divided in two and Ming had stayed with Ivan. Gurav and Tyler worked under a new manager. Gurav and the new guy had a working relationship marked by passive-aggressive behaviors, backstabbing, and resentment. Again, Ming thought, is this a case of office politics—retaliation, retribution, or just plain meanness?

Meanwhile the rest of the employees, upset, had gone into the kitchen to silently spoon ice cream. It was not a good day for morale.

Ming returned to his cube and anxiously sent out a mass email to friends and family. "Given that my office is no longer the friendly place it once was, please send personal e-mails, questionable forwards, and inappropriate jokes to my Yahoo account and *not* to my work account." His work e-mail had been Ming's primary account not only because it had no memory limit but also because it was always open as he worked. He now recognized that there was nothing personal at the office.

Ming realized that the camaraderie of the five-person team in a cramped room was gone forever. But more than that, Gurav was his best friend. He had gotten Ming the job, helped him learn the ropes, was there to help when he was frustrated. Now he was gone and Ming was still there.

"I don't know what the appropriate response to this situation is. Maybe I should quit just to let them know that you cannot treat good people so poorly. Or maybe I should just put in less effort. Or maybe I should do worse. I feel so bad. I would go home but I no longer have a ride."

Myung Jean Chun, a native of Korea, is an assistant producer at Electronic Arts (interactive gaming company) in Walnut Creek, California.

18

The Workplace of Doom

Willa Bruce

My name is Dominic. I am a public servant and I am a bureaucrat. My first day on the job at the Department of Motor Vehicles was about to begin. It was a stormy day. The sky was ominous. Winds gusted and icy rain blew across my windshield as I crept into an already-crowded parking lot.

Regardless of the weather, I was happy and excited. Despite the state's current budget crunch, I had been offered a position higher and better paid than any I had ever had. I would be in charge of developing and implementing new licensing and motor vehicle policies to assist in the prevent-terrorism program of the state. My wife could quit her job and stay home with the baby. I was an executive! We had already bought a new house. It was extravagant, but we could pay for it with my income. I was in seventh heaven. I was whistling and laughing and fantasizing about the wonderful future I had in store.

"This is it," I said to myself. "This job is the reason I got an MPA. I gave up sleep to study for this degree, and this job is the payoff for all my hard work."

I finally found a parking place in the far outreaches of the parking lot as the skies thundered a warning and the lightning sparked. All the rain and the search for a parking place had taken more time than I had planned, so I was a few minutes late as I ran into the building and headed toward the office that would be mine and an appointment with the department's head and my new boss.

A large, imposing man stood in front of my office window, one hand on his hip, one eye on his watch. His red hair was spiked above his white face and his navy blazer was tight across his shoulders. The pointed toes of shiny cowboy boots poked out under his trousers. Because I had listened to my wife's instructions on how to dress for success, I felt out of place.

"I am Melvin Chesterfield McGhee, and you must be Dominic," he said with a saccharine smile, "but my friends call me 'MC.' Welcome to the department." We shook hands as the thunder boomed its warning.

"Damn!" I thought, with a sinking feeling in the pit of my stomach. "This man is my boss, and I have offended him by being late."

"I'm sorry," I stammered. "The storm . . . I got lost . . . I couldn't find parking. . . ."

"Nonsense!" he beamed. "I'm just glad you're here. You must be soaked. And getting lost is a pain, but almost everyone does the first day or two.

"Would you like some coffee or tea? I'll get it for you," he offered, then shouted out the door, "Lisa, would you bring us some coffee, dear?"

I felt like he was going to be a great guy to work for. I again congratulated myself on getting this job.

Boy, was I wrong!

"Where are you living?" he asked as Lisa brought the steaming cups to us.

I started to describe our new dream house, but he interrupted me. "Oh yes, *that* neighborhood! I do hope your family will be safe there. It's not the best part of town. You should have consulted me."

He got up and walked to the window and asked me to join him there.

"See that black BMW convertible parked in the reserved space?" he asked. "That's my new set of wheels. The license plate says 'MC,' for my name of course—Melvin Chesterfield. Some of my staff thought I should have put 'King,' but I prefer 'MC'—that also stands for 'Master of Ceremonies' you know, and I do know how to keep things under control and happening just as I want them to. I am a true master." He then proceeded to tell me about his horse, Stallion, and all the trophies he had won in dressage.

It was almost time for lunch before he stopped talking. He gave me a manual of procedures to read, a list of appointments he had made for me, and, as he left my office, he said, "I'm really glad you're here. You are so smart and capable. I always hire the best, and this time, that is you. I can't wait to show you off."

Again, he smiled the enigmatic smile and was gone. That smile gave me the creeps. His lips moved, but his eyes were cobalt marbles, showing no emotion.

As the days moved into weeks, I felt honored to be MC's protégé. He arranged for my membership in several private, prestigious clubs and insisted that I attend functions with him. My wife was never included. Neither was his. He set up working committees for me to chair. He introduced me to influential people, but he would always conclude the introduction with words like, "Of course, *I* am the head of the department, *he* is only an employee."

I guess I'm slow, but it took me about 6 months to figure out why he really called himself "MC." He was the ultimate manipulator. When committees met, he would always "drop in" and soon take over the meeting, preempting the group agenda with his own. When decisions were made, he would make a speech promoting his own ideas. If I made a suggestion, he would immediately say that was "unworkable." If the committee voted for a solution other than his own, he would call another meeting on the same subject and continue that process until the vote went his way. If he laughed, others could laugh, but woe to the person who laughed when he didn't! Those cobalt eyes bore into my very soul and I became more and more intimidated. He wanted to control my emotions as well as my actions.

I was undermined and devalued and mad. I set up an appointment to discuss my concerns with him, struggling to be objective and point to real problems. The meeting was not productive. He took each issue I raised, twisted it, and declared it a misunderstanding by me. He denied introducing me as "only an employee."

"You've been spending too much time talking to your coworkers," he said. "They're an inept bunch of malcontents." He named a few of my colleagues and told me that he had evidence of their incompetence and that plans were underway to encourage their resignations or transfer.

"That civil service system just gives too much protection. You should just ignore them and do your job and things will all work out. I do have a plan for handling this," he concluded. "Just be careful," he urged, "that you do not become one of them."

And, at first, I believed him. That this many professionals could all be judged "incompetent" now seems farfetched, but after all, MC was in charge, and I thought he should know.

We fell into a kind of daily rhythm, MC and I. If I spoke up, to clarify, explain, or even present evidence to support the policy I was recommending, MC would tell me that I was wasting everyone's time. "You really do not know what you're talking about," he would say. I began to believe him.

My self-confidence faded. If MC walked into a room, I got nauseous. Sometimes I stuttered. I began to think I was dumb. Then a meeting with MC reassured me.

"You've been working very hard," he told me, "and the *company* appreciates it. You have now been here almost a year, and I have recommended you for a 10 percent raise to reward you for all your efforts." Then he smiled his mirthless smile. "See, I do like you and think you are a real asset to our operation," and he invited my wife and me to dinner.

My job felt secure again. I began to relax. MC liked me after all. As I think back, I must have felt a little like a kidnap victim who starts to see the kidnapper as the savior and not the enemy.

Ever the optimist, I threw myself into my work with new vigor. I surveyed other states' department of motor vehicles on their terrorism policies. I prepared reports. I made recommendations for change, as I thought I had been hired to do. I also did as MC said and quit speaking to my coworkers—though we kept our network intact by calling one another on the phone. MC never did catch on to our subterfuge. I made no decision without checking with him first. And I did nothing that he did not ask me to do. I thanked him when he found fault with my work. My initiative and enthusiasm were gone, but I had survived—or so I thought.

MC did not change. His criticism of me turned to rejection. He began to spy on me. I would get a glimpse of his red spiky hair in the hall outside my door or hear his sardonic laughter as he quizzed my secretary about what I did and said. I couldn't understand why he had quit talking with me. I felt undermined and devalued. I worked harder and began smoking again to try to calm my nerves. Rather than denigrate my suggestions, he now simply stayed away from me and never asked for my input. I never knew if I was doing my job or not, but I kept plugging away. MC found fault with everything I said or did. One day, after I had been working for him about 2 years, he told me, "You are simply a square peg in a round hole. I don't have enough evidence to fire you, but I am going to replace you."

My wife is getting fed up with hearing me complain about work; she wants me to quit or at least start looking for another job. But the government still has a freeze on hiring, and the money I am making is more than I have ever earned before. We have debts and that big house payment besides. I couldn't leave. I am now a nail biter and a chain smoker. I dread going to work, and I search the parking lot for that MC license plate so I can park as far away from it as possible. I started seeing a psychotherapist. I cannot sleep. I don't know what to do.

Willa Bruce is professor of public administration at the University of Illinois at Springfield.

PART II

Comments

Case 1 Comments:
Parking Tickets and School Bonds

What Is Wrong and What Should Be Done?

Mel Dubnick

"One thing has nothing to do with another." This is the simple and clear answer to Patricia's dilemma. And a dilemma it is—but the question is, of what type?

At first blush, what Patricia faces might be regarded as one of two types of dilemmas, one political and the other ethical. From this perspective, the political dilemma is whether or not to exercise her discretion in her role as liaison with the media for the purpose of facilitating (or at least not interfering with) an important political objective associated with her role as part of the city's policy-making team. On the ethical side, her dilemma is whether to abuse her role obligations as media liaison in order to accomplish a desirable end: promoting the call for a referendum that she and the policy-making team regard as important and desirable.

Based on more careful consideration, however, it becomes evident that neither of those dilemmas is credible, and that the choice facing Patricia is of a quite different sort. She in fact does not face a political dilemma, for she is not authoritatively empowered with the discretion to delay the media request for information. As a staff professional, Patricia is an agent with obligations—moral as well as legal—to meet the standards of the relevant open-records policies. She is in a position to suggest to someone in an authoritative position under those policies to delay the list's release (e.g., the city attorney or head of the treasurer's office), but in doing so she risks magnifying her error by dragging that individual or office into a conspiracy to undertake an unwarranted violation of the policy. She can avoid that danger only by providing a false justification or rationalization for the delay, but in doing so she is merely sliding down a more personal slippery slope into unethical—and perhaps actionable—conduct.

Nor is her dilemma an ethical one, for ethical dilemmas are by their nature choices between two rights. In ethics there is no question about the choice between doing the right and wrong thing. Even if the referendum were the "ultimate good" for the community's future, violating one's moral and legal obligations to achieve that end is not a question of ethics. Rather, it is a question of strategic calculation: What price, in terms of my willingness to live with the consequences, am I ready to pay in order to secure the positive vote on the referendum? What we have here is not an ethical dilemma, but a decision on whether to cut a Faustian deal by putting one's professionalism on the line.

So it comes down to a different kind of dilemma, one faced by a great many public management professionals who assume multiple role obligations at work. In Patricia's case (as in the case of many others in similar circumstances) it is a dilemma generated by a coincidence of role obligations—it just so happens that she finds herself in a position to abuse one set of role obligations in order to facilitate a positive outcome for another set of role obligations. Under these conditions, the wise course is to remember that wonderful bit of street wisdom: "One thing has nothing to do with another."

Mel Dubnick is a visiting professor and senior fellow at the Institute of Governance, Public Policy and Social Research at Queen's University in Belfast, Northern Ireland.

Yilin Hou

There are two main issues in this case: implementation of the public information act concerning the outstanding unpaid parking tickets in the city of Madison and the referendum on issuing bonds for capital projects at the public schools. On the surface the two issues are detached; however, the case develops with the two interwoven, leading to the classic problem in public administration.

The problem evolves from the public administration and democracy equilibrium. It emerges from the potential "conflict" between the release of public information and the possible "threat" the release might have on an agenda of the city government. Release of public information is a specific reliable measure of democracy, and it is a legal requirement. The conundrum facing the city's public affairs officer is whether she should pursue her long-standing belief in governmental transparency or sacrifice that belief for urgent administrative convenience with the good excuse of the extra few hours being "unreasonable cost" to the city.

If Patricia sticks to her belief, the school bond referendum may once again fail, which is not in the benefit of the city, the school district, or even the residents of the city whose children are in the schools. In this sense, using discretion to bypass the release "could" benefit everyone.

The counterargument can be as strong or even stronger. The large number of unpaid parking tickets reveals inadequate enforcement of existing city ordinances—effectiveness of administration is a problem already. Publishing the database will only serve to provide public supervision that will in turn contribute to improving enforcement. Democracy is no contradiction to public administration. Worries and doubts cannot stand.

Another, though weaker, counterargument may go that though the public affairs officer's concern is not without reason, it may not be necessarily true that revelation of outstanding tickets of the three school board members and a few city officials will derail the referendum. On the contrary, it may remind tax payers again of the importance of the public eye on public affairs and government officials.

A minor problem is (remotely) related to the so-called administration and politics dichotomy. In this context, it is the "loyalty" of public servants to their boss, the person who appointed them. Should Patricia, the public affairs officer, get Harry, the city manager, involved in this issue? If she does, then any possible legal or administrative consequences will expose the city manager. If not, and the release does derail the referendum, then Patricia is not serving her boss well. Should Patricia be neutral on any administrative "politics" and be free of the political appointee mentality to serve nothing else but the best of pure public interest?

Options for Action

Interested readers may be curious as to what Patricia ought to do. It depends. Possible choices follow our interpretations of the situation. She may choose to deny the release of outstanding ticket information; and with an "excusable" excuse of unreasonable cost to the agency, she can be protected against strong legal actions by Maria. Even if the scenario turns sour, her boss is insulated from the issue. If Patricia does this, the referendum may pass without much disturbance.

Another choice is that she follows her administrative neutrality principle: Since the fact is fact, it should be released by the open-information law. This may cause some pressure on those board members and city officials; however, it does not necessarily mean the referendum cannot pass. In fact, with explanation and effective communication with local people, the project proposal may pass. The event itself may well serve dual purposes—to make public figures more vigilant and to remind the general public of the necessity of placing more scrutinizing attention on public affairs.

Yilin Hou, a native of China, teaches public administration at the University of Georgia.

Babette Smit

Patricia should discuss the matter with Harry that afternoon. Before the meeting, Patricia should analyze the dilemma with which she is confronted. On the one hand, great benefit can be derived from Maria's intention to publicize the database, as the added social pressures on big-time offenders first should lead to the payment of the outstanding tickets and second may contribute to better adherence to traffic rules in the future. This will enhance the safety of all citizens in the city. On the other hand, publicizing the names of the school board members at this stage may jeopardize the upcoming school bond referendum. Similarly, publicizing the names of offending city officials can cause damage to the institutional integrity of the city administration and also convince other offenders that tickets need not be paid. However, opting to publicize only the non–public office offenders on the database and not the names of the offending school board members or city officials would imply that public officials are not subject to the same rules as the rest of the citizens in the city. This will also cause much greater damage to the integrity of the administration should this later become public.

That afternoon during the meeting with Harry, after concluding their discussion on the upcoming school bond referendum, Patricia brings up the subject of Maria's request. She explains that it had been a reasonable request and that she has already discussed the legal implications of releasing the data with the city's attorney. She also stresses the importance of a transparent system as one of the key components of good governance. After explaining the advantages and disadvantages of publicizing the database, including the names of the school board members and public officials on the list, she asks Harry whether he supports her intention to release the data. Harry might agree in principle, but emphasizes that he does not want to place the school bond referendum of the following week at risk, especially since it was already narrowly defeated the previous year.

Then, Patricia suggests that they postpone the release of the database for one week until the following Friday. This gives the office of the city manager time to notify the relevant school board members and city officials of the intention to release the data. The affected persons may then choose to either pay their tickets or be subject to the same social pressure as the rest of the persons on the database. Furthermore, it also limits the risk to the upcoming referendum, but keeps in line with the principle of transparent governance and equal treatment.

Upon Harry's acceptance of her proposal, Patricia asks Harry to send urgent personal letters to the school board members and city officials on the list, informing them of the city's intention to release the database by the following Friday. Thereafter she phones Maria and explains that the data are taking longer to redact than originally planned. She apologizes for the delay, but assures Maria that an edited copy of the database will be made available to her by the following Friday.

Babette Smit is a consultant with Unistel Consultus, Stellenbosch University, South Africa.

Case 2 Comments: The Education of the Police Commissioner

What Is Wrong and What Should Be Done?

Richard C. Kearney

Mr. Mayerbeer bravely and patriotically accepted the president's plea to take on an insuperable set of tasks related to building a cohesive national police force out of numerous ethnic and national cultures and combating rampant crime. As CEO of the NPF, Mayerbeer had two and a half years to change cultural attributes that were generations in the making. The endemic problems of ethnic rivalries and widespread crime could not be corrected in such a short period of time by any single individual, no matter how talented, committed, and well connected. Experience and research from many different countries indicate that police activity only affects crime levels at the margins. The human, economic, and societal factors that produce crime are not clearly understood, and what is known about correlates and causes of crime provides little reason to hope that police organizational changes can have much direct impact. Moreover, Mayerbeer entered an organizational environment very different from that of the NAB. A hard-nosed, business approach to reforming a police organization may have had value, but certainly not sufficient value to attain meaningful success. Mayerbeer lacked familiarity and experience with law enforcement, which would impose certain learning and credibility costs on him that would not afflict an experienced police administrator.

Thus, the lack of clearly visible results at the end of Mayerbeer's tenure is understandable. But how should he tackle the written analysis of the past two and a half years so that he, his successor, and the president can learn and adapt?

First, Mayerbeer should reflect in writing on his experiences. He should check his daily calendar to aid his memory of past events and identify key turning points. He should consult individually with his leading NPF administrators and consider asking the president to appoint a blue ribbon commission of top police administrators and business leaders to study the problems of crime and law enforcement and report to the president upon completion of their work. And he should consider a systematic means of gathering input from the rank-and-file police officers.

Simultaneously, Mayerbeer should contract with a sample of the independent researchers who have already written critical reports to advise him about what went right, what went wrong, the reasons for successes and failures, and recommendations for the future. This will give him an unbiased review of his tenure at NPF and assist him in writing his report to the president.

Richard C. Kearney is the chair of the Department of Political Science at East Carolina University in Greenville, North Carolina.

Rosanne Manghisi

Clearly the first problem facing this country is the reduction of serious crime, which is paramount to restoring order and confidence not only for the police but also for the public. The police had become "soldiers" for the government, thereby creating a lack of trust among the citizens, echoed by the words that the police were "feared and resented" by the public. Second, the police themselves lacked leadership and direction. Having a wide array of problems within the police department ranging from corruption, the consolidation of several agencies into one, a new leader with no police background, lack of resources, and high rates of suicide, alcoholism, and absenteeism clearly contributed to the anxiety associated with chaos and change. Last, a new leader arrives, with no known law enforcement background, with a sound reputation in the business world, and a great deal of past successes, yet his private sector success did not transfer to the public sector.

The Solution: Mayerbeer has 6 months left on the job. I suggest that he develop a transition plan for the National Police Force so that the incoming director can begin on a more solid foundation than he did. The plan should be twofold: It should focus on the physical organization of the police department and how it can be structured to most effectively reduce crime; and the plan should focus on the restoration of public confidence in the police, through effective policing and effective communication with the public. Based on his experience of the past year and a half, Mayerbeer's transition plan should include some of the following recommendations:

- Establish meaningful community partnerships. This would be an important first step toward rebuilding trust of the department as well as increasing transparency and accountability.
- Develop a communication strategy. Confidence can only be instilled through clear and effective communication and by taking responsibility for the agency's successes along with its failures.
- Identify someone within the department to handle media communications, essentially a spokesperson for the department who can send a clear and consistent message to the various media outlets.
- Empower personnel to use their authority properly and lawfully to reduce public fear and hold them accountable to the new constitution.
- Adopt the "broken windows" theory of effective policing. The "broken windows" theory states that if law enforcement officials focus on petty crimes and quality of life issues—such as replacing broken windows and

repairing street lights—behavior will change and tolerance for disruptive, disrespectful behavior will diminish as well.

- Provide appropriate training so the police will become more confident in policing.
- Create focus groups or study groups among the police and community to establish open dialogue and engender a cooperative spirit among the police and community. Select a member from the police to serve as a liaison with community leaders to accurately report their concerns.

Mayerbeer's last challenge is to prepare a successor since he knows firsthand the challenges the new director will confront. He needs an exit strategy in order to show his accomplishments for achieving success in accordance with his plan. He needs to take credit for the successes and take responsibility for the failures. In doing so, he needs to offer solutions to improve the agency or a plan to retool the way they do business. He should not leave without a win, or at least a partial win. And he should not leave without providing his successor with a thorough assessment of the agency's strengths and weaknesses and a list of agenda items that the next commissioner should consider addressing.

Rosanne Manghisi is a captain with the New Jersey State Police. She is the first woman from the NJSP to graduate from the FBI National Academy.

Nancy Soper DuBro

It is not enough for new leaders to have strong managerial skills and the ability to create a compelling vision. To successfully navigate the mine-fields of leadership succession and oversee the intricacies of organizational change, new leaders must have in-depth knowledge of the organization's culture, values, and history. Also, they need to establish credibility and earn the trust of the organization very soon after taking the helm. No one pays the price of failed succession like the successor. Such is the case of Mr. Mayerbeer. One minute Mr. Mayerbeer was the highly respected head of a major private sector enterprise expecting to succeed in an organization where his predecessors had failed. Soon thereafter Mr. Mayerbeer had submitted an early resignation to return to the private sector. What went wrong?

One can hardly imagine two more dissimilar organizations than a brewery and a police force, and it follows that the leadership styles must also differ in fundamental ways. In the brewery, workers produce the same product day in and day out according to set formulations and standard operating procedures. Brewery workers carry out their duties within the confines of a factory-type environment characterized by conformity, con-sistency, and repetition and are discouraged from independent thinking. Not so in the case of the police officer, where each day brings new situa-tions and personal risk and requires a high degree of individual judgment in the field. The leadership style necessary to achieve success in a factory envi-ronment where the workers produce the same standardized product each day is not the same leadership style required of the head of a police organi-zation who must have confidence in the ability of officers in the field to deal with ever-changing, unpredictable, critical, and sometimes life-threatening situations. Unfortunately, the sound business practices that served Mr. Mayerbeer well in his brew factory environment are not the same lead-ership skills he needs as the CEO of the NPF. Mr. Mayerbeer's fate was sealed almost from the very beginning.

Despite Mr. Mayerbeer's several significant achievements during his tenure, his accomplishments clearly fell short of expectations. In this situ-ation, Mr. Mayerbeer's first inclination may be to write a final report that is defensive and explains away the reasons for his lack of success. Harvard professor Rosa Melissa Moss Kanter refers to this as "putting lipstick on a bulldog" or, more simply stated, trying to put the best face on a bad situation. Before embarking on the writing of a report that is defensive, self-protective, and implies that the NPF, not Mr. Mayerbeer, is to blame, Mr. Mayerbeer should ask himself the following questions:

- How will the press and politicians use/misuse a report that casts aspersions on the NPF?
- What short-term and long-term effects might this report have on the NPF and the country's citizens?
- How will I feel after I submit such a report?

There is another approach. It is a final report that lays the foundation for a better future for the NPF and serves to advocate much-needed changes. For example,

- Compensation systems that pay police officers competitively
- Encouraging a promote-from-within personnel policy
- Providing the NPF with a budget that gives police officers the equipment and training they need to carry out their duties

In order for organizations to succeed and move forward, employees need to experience a sense of pride and meaning about their work. Public service employees in particular need to feel that they have the power to make a difference in their community, and that they can achieve personal satisfaction by helping their organization and their community succeed. In his farewell statements—both in his final report and his public remarks— Mr. Mayerbeer should thank the staff and officers of the NPF for their support and for a job well done. In addition, Mr. Mayerbeer should acknowledge that it has been an honor for him to serve the fine men and women of the NPF as their CEO. There is much to gain when an executive's voluntary departure from an organization is conducted with dignity by all parties involved. It is not the time for public finger pointing and the placing of blame.

Nancy Soper DuBro, PhD, is an organization development consultant with Universal Technology Corporation, headquartered in Santa Fe, New Mexico.

Case 3 Comments: Community Outreach Chaos

What Is Wrong and What Should Be Done?

Cheryl Simrell King

The Problem(s)

Dr. Schuman is indeed in trouble. Despite her good intentions (and, apparently, the good intentions of the grant), she committed the classic mistake in community development work: She built a process that was expert and institution centered instead of community and citizen centered. This mistake is repeated far too often, for many reasons, not the least of which is the institutional and attitudinal separation between "experts" and citizens played out in situations like this and in "not in my backyard" (NIMBY) movements. A group of, apparently, well-intentioned administrators and experts, assisted by a few community leaders (who are not, necessarily, neighborhood residents), decide what is best for a community and then try to export or sell their ideas to the community.

This story is reminiscent of the aborted beginning of the Dudley Street Initiative in Boston. That initiative began with a group of "outsiders" (some of whom were administrators of community agencies and community leaders, but not neighborhood residents) who invested a great deal of time in determining, without neighborhood or community involvement, the neighborhood problems and solutions. They brought their prepared (and well-funded) plans to the neighborhood and were, in the words of one Boston city administrator, "taken to the wood shed" for doing this work without the involvement of the neighbors.

Dr. Schuman has been taken to the wood shed. She made the grievous error of not engaging the neighborhood from the very beginning and she has to fix this error. In addition, apparently this is not the first time the university approached its community-based work in the same, expert-centric way. Both Dr. Schuman and the university need to consider either changing their ways or getting out of this line of work.

Some other problems:

1. Don't do community-based work if you are looking for accolades and attention. It's better to not do the work at all than to do it for the wrong reasons.

2. Dr. Schuman and her team approached this neighborhood from a needs/deficit approach rather than from an assets/appreciatory approach. This translates to the classic attitudes that folks in marginalized communities are not likely to stand for anymore: "There is something wrong with you and we know what we can do to fix it for you. . . . Oh, and we expect that you'll appreciate us greatly for doing so!" (the so-called great-white hope approach).

3. Race and class are clearly issues, although we are not sure to what degree Dr. Schuman worked to ensure that her team was representative.

The Solution(s)

Tonight

What Dr. Shuman needs to do tonight is to invite the attendees to talk to her, to vent their frustrations, and to talk about their dreams for the future of their neighborhood. She then should step back and listen. Nothing more.

Dr. Schuman should try to communicate two things to the meeting attendees: It is clear to her, after two meetings, that she and her team have acted like "uninvited guests" and they need to be a different sort of guest; and, that she is interested and willing to listen to those assembled regarding how she should go about doing this.

Tomorrow

Dr. Schuman needs to begin working on reconfiguring the project such that is it neighborhood centered, instead of expert and institution centered.

She needs to take what was suggested at the meeting last night and put it into action. She will have to meet with her college administrators and explain how they went wrong and make them aware of the importance of proceeding differently with this work in particular, and with all their community partnership work in general. The college, obviously, needs to work to heal the rift between the community and the college; it will be no small job to convince neighborhood residents that the college is not taking an "ivory tower," privileged approach to this and other work.

Dr. Schuman would be well served to get her hands on materials describing a participatory approach to community development and on materials that explain an asset-based approach toward community development. Dr. Schuman should ask herself if she's got what it takes to do this work well—if not, she needs to consider finding a suitable replacement. Ultimately, she needs to reconfigure her approach such that she and her team are working for the neighborhood, instead of the other way around.

Cheryl Simrell King is a member of the faculty of The Evergreen State College in Olympia, Washington.

Lyle Wray

Dr. Schuman has several serious problems. The essence of what lies before her are the steps needed to recover trust and build sufficient legitimacy for the project and its goals to proceed. In 20/20 hindsight, more direct involvement of the leaders and community members from the specific part of the community to be involved in the project, with intense listening to their concerns and desires would be a good foundation. The next step would be to reach out to college members who could advise her on just who the community leaders in census tract 16 are, on strategies for connecting with the leaders, and on helping set up a "recovery" plan. One unpleasant and ego-deflating step for Dr. Schuman would be to try to work to set up a small meeting with key community leaders in census tract 16 and to lay out a candid *mea culpa* of failures to involve the affected community directly and deeply at the beginning, to listen to community concerns, and to have the community help shape the grant.

The challenge then would be to identify the nature of a "win-win" for the community and the project going forward around the common ground of attempting to improve the community. She might suggest and then hear feedback on steps to prevent communications failures and to ensure that the community and its leaders get credit equal to or greater than college academics. In sum, the problem was a failure to build legitimacy and communication with the affected community. The challenge Dr. Schuman faces is to take steps to discover, if possible, common ground and to build a win-win situation going forward for the college and the community to carry out the COPC project and to meet concerns of community members.

Lyle Wray is the director of the Ventura County Civic Alliance in Camarillo, California. He provides technical assistance in Singapore, Malaysia, Hong Kong, and Macau on strategies for building Web-enabled government and on outcomes measurement. In addition, he worked on civic engagement initiatives in Thailand, Armenia, and Korea.

Kaifeng Yang

The problem here is about an academician entering the real world of citizens, politicians, and media: What Dr. Schuman needs is not only enthusiasm and knowledge, but also planning and strategies. She has made many mistakes that led to the fiasco she is now facing. For example, the grant requirements stated that the program "should address the expressed needs of the urban community," and "the residents themselves should identify community needs." However, instead of appealing directly to citizens, Dr. Schuman relied on the politically selected steering committee to both select the neighborhood and to decide on the needs to address. Local political leaders were given the majority of the credit for the award. The result is an alienated community and polarized resistance from the residents.

The first thing Dr. Schuman should do is to reflect on herself, change her attitude, and seek some help. She needs to find somebody who really understands local politics, public relations, and implementation of community development programs. She may find some help from public administration or social work departments of the college, or from outside consulting firms and nonprofit organizations.

The grant program strategy must be completely revised, and new leadership must be installed from the community to instill a sense of fairness and equity to the equation. Before arranging more workshops, Dr. Schuman has to communicate with local activists including Rhonda Howard, with the Montville chapter of the NAACP, and with other community or neighborhood organizations. A meeting should then be arranged with these activists and organizations, the steering committee, the mayor, other elected officials, the local media, and the college administrators. The meeting should result in a new implementation committee that includes more African Americans and more nonpolitical members.

This more representative implementation committee should replace the steering committee and take responsibility for the program from this point on. Within the committee, open lines of communication and a system of accountability should be established. There needs to be professional financial administration of the grant so that all questions can be answered and sufficient oversight maintained. To make the new committee possible and effective, facilitation and coordination skills are essential.

A citizen survey could be administered, with the participation of the local media, to communicate the benefits and purposes of the program to the residents, and to collect the residents' opinion on what the community needs really are and how the grant program should be run. The survey process can serve as an opportunity to appease the grumbles, show the organizers' authenticity, and engage more residents.

The cooperation of the local media is very important. The media can be your best friend or your worst enemy. They need some involvement in the grant program so that they can identify with it and develop a desire to see it succeed. The residents need to be given the limelight and credit for tackling the needs of the community and working with the available resources in the town to address and solve those needs.

Kaifeng Yang, a native of China, teaches public administration at Florida State University.

Case 4 Comments: Performance Reports

What Is Wrong and What Should Be Done?

Maria P. Aristigueta

Mr. Ndlovu, municipal manager of Sunnyview, has to present a quarterly report to the regional council. Although there are plenty of performance data available, there is significant disagreement among the senior management team on what is to be reported.

In analyzing the case, we notice certain facts: Each of the service managers reports that they are doing their best within the limited budgets available to them. A large number of vacancies are affecting performance. The press and the citizens have been raising some critical issues including poor quality of service delivery, increase in crime, high levels of child abuse, lack of government-subsidized housing, and inadequate infrastructure for water and electricity. Internal management problems in the form of bureaucratic delays in obtaining approval for expenditures on project changes are also creating problems.

The assumption being made in the case is that the council will want to have all of these issues addressed in this quarterly report. Mr. Ndlovu as the municipal manager needs to provide structure on what will be reported to the council, and there are some unknowns in this case. For example, does the municipality have a strategic plan? If so, what is the mission of the municipality? We see two goals in the case study: to insure safety and to improve the quality of life. Are there other goals? There is discussion of performance data; are the performance data related to performance measures in support of goals or objectives? Taking into account the unknown, two separate scenarios are offered.

Scenario 1: If the answer is yes to strategic planning—mission, goals, and performance measures—then I would suggest that Mr. Ndlovu produce a report addressing the performance indicators as established through the strategic planning process. Issues that fall outside the strategic plan should be addressed at a separate meeting. For example, if reduction in crime is a performance indicator under the goal of ensuring safety, I would report the reduction in murder rate and reported rapes and the increase in burglaries. Explanations should be provided in the report including the limitations of a police department on crime statistics that are influenced by societal factors such as unemployment and poverty.

Scenario 2: If the answer is no to strategic planning, then Mr. Ndlovu is left with the dilemma of less structure in which to report the accomplishments and shortcomings. A viable possibility would be for Mr. Ndlovu to report the problems in terms of internal and external factors affecting the municipality. For example, internal problems include the high turnover of staff and the shortage of employees. External assumptions include that the larger municipalities and private businesses are poaching the experienced staff members by offering higher wages and better benefits. Mr. Ndlovu could recommend that the council approve a comprehensive management analysis or evaluation to determine the actual cause of the turnover.

In closing, Mr. Ndlovu should establish a reporting mechanism for the quarterly reports that he presents to the regional council. Service area managers can provide assistance by reporting their activities and achievements, and this is most useful if it is aligned with the municipality's goals and objectives as was described under Scenario 1. If Sunnyview has not undergone a strategic planning process, it should be high on the list of Mr. Ndlovu's recommendations to the council. The strategic planning process should be facilitated by someone with expertise in the area. For this quarterly report, Mr. Ndlovu will then need to report activities and achievements that may be structured as described under Scenario 2.

Maria P. Aristigueta teaches policy analysis and evaluation at the University of Delaware and is currently working with the Instituut voor de Overheid - K.U. Leuven, Belgium, on national efforts to implement performance management.

Andrew Bednarek

Mr. Ndlovu, the municipal manager of Sunnyview, has found himself in the "eye of the storm" and he has himself to thank for his current condition. The internal and external problems listed below did not just start in the last quarter of Mr. Ndlovu's 2-year tenure as a manager.

Internal	External
Organizational politics	High levels of child abuse
Charges of political interference	Lack of government-subsidized housing
Bureaucratic delays/ineptitude	Year after year increase in crime
High staff turnover	High unemployment
Shortage of employees	Housing project delays
Limited budgets	Inadequate infrastructure
Poaching of trained employees by private organizations	Negative publicity from community stakeholders
Lack of consensus of senior staff relative to performance baselines	City services impeded by danger of crime
An attitude of "doing best we can"	Squatters illegally occupying housing
	Quality of life in Sunnyview needs improving

It appears that the issues are reaching critical mass. As the city manager, he has an opportunity to demonstrate his leadership and managerial skills by presenting his analysis of how internal organizational and managerial problems are trending and ultimately impacting on external communitywide issues. He also has the responsibility to present his quarterly performance data in an honest and objective manner, however unflattering.

The regional council should be looking to management for results. Any performance measurements should be based on a collaborative approach with the community, elected officials, department heads, staff, and the stakeholders, and the approach should not be a punitive process. As such, there is plenty of blame to spread around if the "blame games" begin.

However, if each director is simply reporting that he or she are "doing the best they can" without describing his or her achievements, it is time to start looking for results-oriented managers. Quality organizations set service standards in order to know what to measure and make the distinction between measuring performance and describing activities. It is a validation of performance, or lack of it. Healthy organizations are adaptive and build partnerships with employees, community stakeholders, and the public sector.

As the city manager, I would take some immediate steps with the public safety director to handle the problem of trash collection, assigning a squad to escort the solid waste collectors so trash could be collected. Furthermore, I would do community outreach along with deploying police resources into neighborhoods to find out what is causing the increase in crime. Pertaining to the issues of child endangerment and abuse, I would enlist the support and partner with county and state health officials along with city law enforcement to facilitate the investigation, assessment, and prosecution of child abuse cases. Finally, I would enter into interlocal agreements with other public, charitable, and religious housing shelter programs within the tri-county area and begin to relocate squatter families to adequate shelters. In addition, I would enlist the support of the local volunteer in medicine program to do medical assessments on the squatter population.

Andrew Bednarek is the business administrator for the Borough of Avalon, New Jersey.

Harry J. Hayes

Mr. Ndlovu's tenure as municipal manager appears to be short-lived. After 2 years on the job, even the most basic administrative controls and teamwork have not been put in place. The senior management team is not working off the same sheet of music, nor are they doing any cross communication or partnering to solve the ever building problems facing the city. That a performance report must be submitted to the regional council only highlights the failings of the manager and his senior leadership team. Mr. Ndlovu is indeed facing a turning point as municipal manager.

In my opinion, Mr. Ndlovu needs to request a 1-month delay in making the quarterly report to the regional council. His stated reason should be that he has determined that the current report format does not give a realistic picture of issues facing the municipality and region.

Mr. Ndlovu's next step should be to corral his senior staff for a weekend management retreat and settle the issue of management direction, leadership values, teamwork that crosses departmental lines, and finally, performance initiatives. If more than one weekend session is needed, then so be it. He must get the point across that business as usual is no more.

In his management retreat meetings, Mr. Ndlovu should set strict standards on what he will and will not accept from his leadership team: primarily, complaining about what's wrong as opposed to offering solutions to the problems (opportunities for success) that face the respective departments, the municipality, and the region. The department heads should have no doubt that he expects them to be the "leaders" and "chief cheerleaders" of their areas and departments and if they don't believe that they can do the job, then they should seek other employment.

Once this centerpiece of the administration's report to the regional council is completed, Mr. Ndlovu and his team should have a comprehensive and performance management–centered report of all current issues that confront the administration. The council will be able to effectively see how well or poorly the administration is responding to issues and trends.

Mr. Ndlovu will surely face some heat from the council when he presents the new, "truthful" report. In the long run, however, I believe the council will applaud his leadership and courage for tossing back the covers on the issues that exist in the community.

Harry J. Hayes is the division manager for human resources, safety and benefits for the City of Houston, Texas, Department of Solid Waste Management. He is a former army officer who specialized in human resources and training issues.

Case 5 Comments: The Price of Rebuilding a War-Torn Town

What Is Wrong and What Should Be Done?

Eve Annecke

What to do now? Either focusing solely on rebuilding the factory or moving to another town would clearly mean giving up on the critical moment where a reconciliation process could become part of the town's healing.

Maria needs to take a process approach to building consensus around her challenge. Taking on board the various suggestions within her own organization, she needs to address with her staff the various suggestions they made. She needs to integrate the first two suggestions and point out that while they may yet end up moving their work into another town, she feels this should be their alternative only after they have given their best shot to a way of bringing resettlement and reconciliation into the economic project. She needs to help her staff, and herself, see that the mayor's refusal is a blessing so early on—as it is holds a role for what is very present in the town, that is, massive antagonism toward the refugees. But this is not the only role, or "voice," in the town.

Maria then needs to rapidly meet with other stakeholders, organizations, and more moderate politicians, keeping the project of rebuilding the factory foremost in peoples' minds. She needs to enthusiastically discuss the promise of activity, jobs, economic development, and resettlement. In these meetings Maria needs to also quietly assess the attitude among the different individuals and groups as to the significance of this project and to the possibility of beginning the process of resettlement and reconciliation. She could use stories of other towns or war-torn countries where this has happened, thereby developing a sense of hope and renewal. She could use these meetings to point out that the process would be tough and challenging but that isolating or alienating the refugees would only move and delay, and possibly exacerbate, the problem for the town, and in fact for the entire country. In addition, Maria needs to meet with the refugee leader. She now understands that there is no quick fix to her previously simplistic, rational, deal-making approach and that she needs his help to strategically attempt to slowly and painfully reintegrate the town through the rebuilding of the factory. The chances of moving the refugees back in at this point in time are slim.

In these meetings Maria needs to generate an understanding of the different roles and voices in the town. One is pro-job/pro-economic development. Another is of bringing the refugees back in immediately. The opposite view is to alienate refugees and never allow them to return. Most importantly, it would seem that Maria needs to maintain some level of neutrality and that she cannot merely continue in her previously dualistic, either/or approach. She should not target the mayor as her enemy. She needs him to successfully implement this project. She should avoid setting people up against each other.

Her sole aim in these conversations is to bring all the players into one room, including the mayor. Perhaps she should acknowledge her own naivety to him and apologize to him for her exclusionary approach. It would be wise if she could help the mayor see and understand the potential he has to exercise profound leadership within the town at a crucial time. Perhaps, through her conversations with others, she will find additional people in positions of power and invite them to participate in the process. The point is for Maria to fine-tune her focus on the process and to trust this process. Through dialogue, creating space for peoples' stories, and keeping focused on the possibility of rebuilding their town as a beacon of hope in war-torn times, Maria's communication with stakeholders possessing opposing views has the potential of building a deeper wisdom and strength within the community. However, there is no predictable outcome to this framework—what is required is an understanding of complexity, patterns, and transformation. And patience.

Eve Annecke is a member of the Sustainability Institute of South Africa, an international living and learning center for studies in ecology, communication, and spirit.

Phil Morgan

Important assumptions that can be derived from the narrative are (a) Maria is a foreigner, at least not a member of any of the contending ethnic or "national" groups in the setting; (b) the donors are also foreigners; and (c) Maria and her organizational colleagues propose to change the mission of their organization, from one of emergency/survival services to economic development assistance *and* conflict resolution.

Maria should pursue a two-track strategy.

1. Economic Assistance

The organization should undertake a thorough assessment of the market for the furniture products and the competitiveness of the production process that will replace the former one before they actually commit to rehabilitating the old furniture factory. It is one thing to decide to change direction toward economic development assistance. Given the opportunity cost of reviving the former factory, as opposed to embarking on an entirely new job creation venture(s), the NGO needs to be sure that the furniture factory represents a robust and enduring economic entity. If the rehabilitation of the factory turns out not to be cost effective, those resources should be used to foster other economic ventures that will employ people in the community. That option will also require strategic assessment and should be linked with the region beyond the town itself. (It must be remembered that in a globalizing economy, furniture is no longer a labor-intensive process, unless it is of hand-crafted custom design.)

As the NGO embarks on a new direction of economic assistance it is important to remember that such organizations have very limited capital. Therefore, in coming to grips with factory rehabilitation versus other ventures, the "other ventures" have to be wealth creating enterprises that require very modest capital inputs. In other words, an NGO getting into economic assistance might well need to think twice about underwriting or contributing to a single venture. Rather, there might be a larger multiplier for the NGO, and the community, if it fostered a microfinancing institution—a type of "bank" dedicated to very small loans to support both "sure-thing" and more entrepreneurial ventures. Investing in many entities that create a few jobs each might be a better risk than betting the bank on one venture/employer.

2. Conflict Resolution

Simultaneously with the above assessments of how best to employ limited resources for economic assistance, the NGO will need to foster a broad community consultative process relating to conflict management. It is evident that Maria was not focused during the emergency services phase on the bitterness of the ethnic conflict. Her clumsy challenge to the mayor revealed that her political welcome could be at risk. Therefore, Maria needs to build on the more positive—even if somewhat skeptical—findings of the survey the NGO had done earlier in the community. She has to find a way to convey those skeptical but willing sentiments of the town's people to the local politicians. There is clearly a gap between community sentiment as revealed in the survey and the mayor's categorical position that all those who left and now want to return are "enemies."

As in doing the economic assessment suggested above, the skills involved in taking on conflict resolution as an additional mission for the NGO might not be readily extant in the organization. Somehow those new skills need to be brought into the organization. During the course of the survey the NGO staff might well have identified selected citizens who were more conciliatory than others, more articulate than others, more well-liked than others, and so on. The NGO could go back to that selected group and discuss ways in which they could signal their own town council persons, political party figures, teachers, clerics, and the like that the citizenry is perhaps more open to discussing ways in which the refugees could return than the mayor and his own group of supporters think. Such skills of mobilization, negotiation, and dispute resolution may have to be "imported" with NGO support.

In sum, the fact that the NGO recognizes that its previous mission can no longer be the centerpiece of its contribution is a sign of organizational learning. However, taking on new tasks—especially those as ambitious as *both* economic assistance and dispute resolution—requires strategic planning, especially an "environmental scan"—or a genuine incorporation of the facts of both the economic and social circumstances. Only then can one weigh the possible effectiveness of launching new initiatives.

Phil Morgan is a professor, and former dean, of the Monterey Institute of International Studies in Monterey, California.

Lyuba Palyvoda

There are several problematic issues facing Maria:

- First of all, it looks like Maria's nongovernmental organization lacks a clear strategy. At the same time, it looks like Maria and her NGO had set very big objectives without carefully analyzing implementation issues. Or, as people say, it is impossible to eat a whole loaf of bread without cutting it into small pieces first. I would add that strategies and tactics for its cutting are important as well.
- Second, communication between Maria's group and the local politicians and governmental officials was woefully inadequate.
- Third, Maria had only one plan: The project was to be implemented in exchange for the return of the refugees. She had only that one idea; nothing else was ready to be put on the table.
- Furthermore, her meeting with the mayor demonstrated that she lacks presentation skills.

In the current situation, I would advise Maria not to be too upset because many organizations working at the community level sooner or later find themselves in such a situation. However, it is very important to spend some time analyzing the current situation and understanding what mistakes were made and to take remedial action to improve organizational operations and then move ahead.

First of all, it seems to me that it will be good for Maria and her organization to conduct organizational strategic planning. I suggest that they

- look back on organizational history, actions, missions, and priorities and analyze their strengths and weaknesses;
- analyze threats and opportunities that exist in the external environment, which includes local community, local government, politicians, and local and international organizations;
- develop detailed strategies and tactics for future activities with actual plans to involve external parties such as community groups, local government, politicians, and businesses.

Second, in the current situation it is important to work directly with the community. I believe that the needs assessment has identified other important issues, and Maria just has to look at its results again. Maria has already noticed that tolerance is a very important issue, and community members and representatives of local government definitely lack it.

Third, Maria's NGO needs to establish a new priority list. This is why it is necessary to involve the community and to make sure that organizational priorities reflect the priorities of the community. Or, in other words, it is important to develop community ownership.

Fourth, I would not initiate direct contact with the mayor or any other local government officials until strong community support and ownership of the new organizational priorities are developed. I would work toward a situation where the community pressures the mayor in order to get him to do what they want.

Finally, my personal recommendation to Maria will be the following: Compromises are good and very useful, but not on important and crucial issues. To my mind, her vision of rebuilding the factory in exchange for the return of the refugees is unacceptable. Certain issues could not be compromised even with the greatest intentions.

Lyuba Palyvoda has more than 10 years of experience in working with NGOs in Ukraine, Moldova, and Belarus. She is presently getting her PhD in Public Administration at Rutgers University while continuing to consult with NGOs in Ukraine. She is director of Counterpart Creative Center in Kiev.

Case 6 Comments: University Games

What Is Wrong and What Should Be Done?

Jacques Bojin

It is obvious that Melissa can talk to Evan without any hesitation because he is her boss as well as Stefan's. Discussing her views on how to promote the university is part of her job. It is also obvious, however, that there are a lot of touchy issues here, because she needs the cooperation and means of the communications office to do her job well.

On the other hand, it's not very fair to say that Stefan's office "should be doing more to promote the university and the city of Alexandria" because they are underfunded and understaffed (probably not Stefan's fault), and public relations is not the major part of their mission. If we had a job definition for Stefan's office, it would probably say something like preparing brochures and catalogues, answering journalists' queries, and so on; things that, apparently, they are doing well and swiftly. The need for proactive PA was not felt until recently, and the university hired Melissa for it.

Melissa has made two mistakes:

1. Attacking the communications office's job head-on. She should have first described her objectives, how she thought the job ought to be done, the means that would be necessary; and this in such a way that it would have then been obvious that the communications office could not provide the help needed. In doing this, she would have demonstrated that she had a clear vision as well as the will and capacity to take on bigger responsibilities.

2. Accepting the offer to meet Stefan to tell him about the project. That's Evan's job.

From a management point of view, Evan also made two big mistakes:

1. Following his meeting with Melissa, he should have held a meeting with both Melissa and Stefan. During that meeting, he would have listened to both of them (first Melissa explaining her project for a print publication, then Stefan's reaction to it) and asked them to cooperate on the project.

2. Evan should never have told Melissa that he would demote Stefan and make him a staff member reporting to her. After all, he is an intelligent and experienced professional, whose only fault is being a bit "sleepy" (maybe because his boss did not know how to "wake him up").

Stefan's reaction on the phone is normal. Now that the harm is done, it's tough to save the situation, especially in view of the fact that it would certainly be bad for the university to lose a professional, or at least diminish his motivation to work.

In my view, Melissa should

1. meet with Stefan to discuss her ideas and enlist his cooperation on the project,

2. highlight the fact that it would be a joint project between Public Relations and Communications, and

3. sugarcoat the whole thing by saying how happy and excited she is to work with a seasoned professional like Stefan.

Then if the project is successful, Melissa may get the promotion, especially if she can claim the major share of the credit for its success. If Stefan is wise, however, he will design a strategy of his own to guard against Melissa's predatory behaviors.

Jacques Bojin is a management consultant living and working in France. He specializes in corporate strategy. He started with McKinsey & Company, then became CEO of a large industrial company before starting his own consulting firm in Paris.

Fanie Cloete

The main problem here is the fact that Melissa was ambitious, overconfident, and overenthusiastic and went over the head of Stefan to his supervisor to discuss desired changes in Stefan's unit without consulting him. She probably did that because she was not impressed with the way in which Stefan ran his unit, and instinctively, or deliberately, sought the ear of the person who was in a position to change things, namely his supervisor, Evan. Evan is sympathetic toward her proposal, but forced her to cooperate with Stefan.

Melissa now has three options:

Option 1: She has now realized that the project is more complex than she had originally anticipated. She could decide to cancel her meeting with him that evening and back out of the project. It would cut her losses, although it would leave her with egg on her face, perpetuate the inefficiencies in Stefan's unit, and blot her budding career at the university. This option would constitute an embarrassing end to her idea but would extricate her from potential conflict with Stefan that could also spill over into her current work situation. This option, however, seems to be a last ditch, fallback position to be avoided at all costs.

Option 2: She can try to calm Stefan down to get his cooperation on the project, as requested by Evan; otherwise she will fail in her bid to take over Stefan's unit if Evan maintains his demand that she cooperate with Stefan. To do this she would have to convince Stefan that she did not try to go over his head, but that she intended only to have an impulsive brainstorming session with Evan about this bright idea that she got, and that he took her by surprise by requesting more details and eventually a concrete proposal. She could explain that she decided to first gauge what Evan's reaction was before contacting Stefan about it. Evan, however, apparently preempted her by contacting Stefan before she could get around to it. She would value Stefan's cooperation, as a result of his experience in that field, and would like his comments on the proposal, as well as his suggestions to improve on it. She could emphasize that the project could only succeed with his assistance and that the university and both of them could gain major benefits from it. If this approach persuades him to join the project, it would overcome the stumbling block, but she would have to keep him committed to the project or face failure as a result of his withdrawal at a later stage or even open resistance and sabotage.

Option 3: This option is to also cancel the meeting with Stefan and go back to Evan with the conclusion that Stefan's involvement with the project will lead to failure similar to his other projects, and maybe even as a result of open hostility to it, leading to probable sabotage attempts. She therefore requests permission to do it without his assistance. If she succeeds on her own, Stefan would be forced to acknowledge her success and her leadership of his unit. This option could, however, also be pursued after the discussion with Stefan, if that did not work out as anticipated.

Melissa's choice of strategy will probably depend on her assessment of how flexible or rigid both Evan and Stefan are. However, my recommendation is that she pursue Option 2. She started down this path and she should see this through. She should work hard to collaborate with Stefan and deliver a top-notch marketing plan for the university. Once that is done, the decision of what to do next is in Evan's hands.

Fanie Cloete teaches public administration at the University of Stellenbosch, South Africa.

Susan Morley

Melissa has really gotten herself into an ethical dilemma. Although she has experience promoting the arts in Alexandria, Melissa appears to have made assumptions that because she was involved in public relations activities in the community, the issues facing Northern U and the dynamics of working at Northern U would be similar to those she faced in her previous position. Because of Melissa's desire to move into a higher position, Melissa went directly to Stefan's supervisor, Evan, voicing concerns and complaints about his performance and his department's inactivity. Hearing what she interpreted to be a sympathetic ear in Evan, she went so far as to indicate she would like Stefan's job. Although Melissa knew from previous experience that "the window dressing may not come close to telling the story," Melissa hadn't taken the time to apply this principle and understand the challenges of working at the university and what factors (underfunding? understaffing?) might be preventing Stefan and his department from being more innovative and proactive in their work.

Because Melissa was so intent on promoting herself and manipulating the situation for her own professional advancement, Melissa seems to have missed some critically important red flags in her discussion with Evan.

• Evan's call to Melissa, suggesting that she propose a project for her and Stefan to work together on, should have struck Melissa as an odd approach showing a lack of leadership and direction from Evan.

• Evan, as supervisor, should have discussed his interest in a joint project between Stefan and Melissa with Stefan directly. Evan put Melissa in the position of notifying Stefan of this (and Melissa accepted this role). Again, Evan's role as a leader is questionable.

• Evan suggested that if this one project went well, Melissa would be considered for Stefan's position. If Evan was ready to promote Melissa after one successful project (and demote Stefan), what type of advocate could Evan be for his employees or their respective departments? Melissa should expect to receive this same lack of support if she worked directly for Evan.

• Melissa should have also immediately been aware that a university administrator cannot even imply that he or she will take these types of personnel actions. Such statements disregard university policies on hiring, promotion, discipline/demotion (and perhaps others such as affirmative action). Evan's "suggestion" that these actions might occur opened Northern U up to employee relations claims from both Melissa and Stefan.

- Melissa should have immediately realized that Evan's suggestion that Stefan report to Melissa is so fraught with problems that even though Melissa missed the other red flags Evan waved at her, this statement alone should have caught her attention. The chance that the long time Communications Director would be demoted and agree to work for the newcomer, Melissa, is slim to none.

Melissa is in a jam. Of course Stefan would question why Melissa, rather than Evan, called to say that they were to work collaboratively on a project. Stefan is immediately suspicious, and with good reason. Melissa should have anticipated this reaction from Stefan. Melissa has been naïve to accept Evan's remarks as real possibilities. Perhaps the light bulb will go off for Melissa that there is more here than meets the eye. Melissa needs to act with integrity and put the best interest of Northern U before her own professional goals. Melissa can possibly salvage the situation by putting her personal agenda aside and see working with Stefan as an opportunity for her to learn from Stefan about the challenges his department faces and the dynamics of working at Northern U. Melissa could then respond to Stefan by stating that although she has public relations and marketing skills from the nonprofit world, she wants to better understand how to use these skills in the university environment, and had therefore suggested the collaborative project. Once she and Stefan begin working together, Melissa is likely to be surprised at what she learns about Evan. Perhaps the problem isn't with Stefan but in fact with the senior administrator's lack of leadership. And perhaps next time, Melissa will attempt to understand the dynamics of the situation before attempting to undermine a coworker for her own personal gain.

Susan Morley is the director of human resources for the Northern Arizona Regional Behavioral Health Authority in Flagstaff, Arizona.

Case 7 Comments:
Redevelopment and the Community

What Is Wrong and What Should Be Done?

Jennifer Brinkerhoff and Derick Brinkerhoff

Sipho's problem is that his Slovo Park constituents depend on the informal economy to generate the resources to sustain their recent socioeconomic advances. The interests of the better-off among Marconi Beam residents are clearly outlined in the agreements made to eventually demolish Cukutown. However, the economic connection between Slovo Park and Cukutown appears to have been unnoticed or ignored in the original negotiations. Now the urban elites want to enforce the agreement, backed up by the power of the police.

So where to from here? Sipho has 3 weeks to design a strategy—hopefully a preemptive one that would avert a role for enforced demolition led by police. The case leaves us with him weighing two options: (a) initiate a dialogue and negotiations with the shebeen owners and the likes of gangsters like Buli or (b) approach NGOs and other development actors with the hope of establishing a viable job and wealth creation strategy. Sipho's choice is not between one or the other of these options, but how to combine the two.

Job creation is a long-term and complicated endeavor. It can rarely reach all of those in need and, it must be recognized, gangsters would have little incentive to participate in formal employment that would likely discriminate against them anyway, given their reputation, dress, and drug habits; nor would formal employment be likely to provide a competitive source of income to deter them from illegal activity. For shebeen owners, job creation might be helpful but would need to be targeted (a challenge in itself) and sufficiently diverse so as not to create debilitating competition in a different market. Job creation addresses only the supply side, not the demand side. Without addressing the demand side, the incentive for others to enter the shebeen business as current owners re-tool remains. Finally, looking to NGOs and developers could be seen as another attempt to bring in top-down externally driven development agendas, undermining the participatory partnership, however imperfect, that initiated the development in Marconi Beam. All that said, job and wealth creation from an expanding set of economic alternatives is the long-term solution for residents of both Marconi Beam and Milnertown.

Sipho seems to genuinely believe in the participatory approach to date. He understands his constituents and he has proven himself to be an effective intermediary, as evidenced by his understanding of the real incentives at play and the contacts he has in the community. These characteristics enable him to engage effectively with all the actors involved, including shebeen owners and the other residents of Slovo Park, Phoenix, and Milnerton. Sipho will need to use his understanding and the trust he has built up to convince the shebeen owners and new Slovo Park residents of the pressing need to identify alternatives to maintaining their economic roots in Cukutown.

Sipho and his community partners need to develop a strategy that explicitly recognizes the economic realities of what it means to move into Slovo Park. They face what is in essence a sequencing problem: how to get from the current situation to a future state where jobs can effectively create sufficient wealth both to provide incomes and support the tax base for local services. Sipho, along with his community partners and local government officials (whom Sipho appears not to have talked to), needs to develop a programmatic vision to present at the upcoming forum meeting that will appeal to all actors, including Harry and other members of the business sector. This program should include new mechanisms for affordable housing finance, low-cost housing construction techniques to reduce the expense of home ownership/rent, integrated skills upgrading and job training, targets for local businesses on employment generation and social responsibility, financial incentives for business investment in the settlement area, community participation with local government for local services provision and financing (water, sewage, trash collection, roads, police, health, education, youth intervention, etc.), and policy dialogue on intergovernmental transfers and tax policy. Such a vision, which explicitly recognizes the steps needed to move forward rather than glossing over the economic role of Cukutown, offers the possibility that the forum meeting will be a productive interchange among the stakeholders, rather than an exercise in confrontation.

Marconi Beam and Milnertown are a microcosm of South Africa's complex and inherently conflictual social, economic, and racial dynamics. Sipho faces enormous challenges in bringing together actors with world-views and motivations as different as Harry's and Buli's while dealing with his own personal ambivalence about being dependent upon elites to provide resources for problem-solving. A shared vision of what is required to make improvements cannot, in and of itself, span these divides, but it is a necessary element to identifying concrete points where interests converge and cooperation can emerge.

Jennifer Brinkerhoff is an associate professor at George Washington University, Washington, DC.

Derick Brinkerhoff is a researcher with the Research Triangle Institute, Washington, DC.

Vache Gabrielian

The problem is that "a complex partnership between central government, local government, private-sector developers, NGOs, and community groups was established to supervise the development of the area." Unfortunately, we do not know exactly what the arrangements of this complex partnership are, nor do we understand the relationship of the many stakeholders, so it raises numerous questions. How many partners have ongoing commitments (are they overcommitted and will they back out?)? How many have only the posture of righteous indignation but neither the leverage nor commitment to bring about change? How many have the expectations of benefits only, without any contribution? Is there a coordinator? How does the government see its role—active, passive, proactive, or reactive? Also, we do not know exactly where the money is coming from and where it is going, what the magnitude of the resources is, or what influence the actors have on the money flow.

As I understand it, there are some loose ends that should be tied up. People living in Slovo Park are not demolishing their shacks and shebeens once they move out, but instead are keeping them. Well, nobody is willing to give up their property easily. Here the program can be amended to address the issue, either by beefing up the funding (if it is viable) or restructuring the schedule of people moving from Cukutown to Slovo Park (i.e., temporarily diverting the funding from new dwellings to other supporting programs). The issue can be addressed in three main ways:

1. The destroying of shacks should not be voluntary, but a condition for moving to Slovo Park.

2. When shacks are destroyed, *something* should take their place, otherwise other shacks will immediately be built in their place. This *something* should either be a legal business or activity, with clearly identified and enforceable property rights, or a long-term government-sponsored project (e.g., building some high-cost public good, such as a hospital, a school, or a stadium). The government commitment, not only the actual construction and building but also the timely completion, should be both secured and clearly communicated to all parties.

3. All of the above-mentioned should be tied to income sustainability, first of all, through employment and training for employment, as well as attracting businesses and NGOs to the neighborhood.

Of course, what is written above is easier said than done, but one should start somewhere.

Assess the situation. How explosive is it? Can it be amended by a "band-aid" approach for a while, while a long-term solution is worked out? What are some intermediate steps that can be taken immediately?

Sipho should have some type of solution for replacing the shacks. His solution should be tangible, possibly encouraging some businesses that will help the low-to-middle-income residents in Slovo Park establish themselves there. Government incentives, such as free land or utilities, might encourage business owners who are hesitant to make the move. At this point in time it is critical that Sipho's approach be viable and tangible. People need to see results, since many promises or assumed consequences of the project did not come true.

Sipho should promote the idea by selling it first to the power brokers and then all the involved parties until it is widely adopted. He may work with the political powerbrokers to get a commitment from the government and/or international donors to support a public works project that will benefit all members of the community. Even the perception that something is being done is often enough to temporarily halt the conflicts. Sipho must continue his promotion of his development ideas until the idea is shared and some action is taken that reflects the democratic reforms that have taken place in this country.

Vache Gabrielian is a board member of the Central Bank of Armenia and a visiting assistant professor at American University of Armenia and Yerevan State University.

Adriaan Schout

Sipho realizes that the situation is heading toward the breaking point. The plans that had been made so far are fine and more or less seemingly created a situation where all parties appeared to be satisfied based on agreements and promises. At some point, however, things can go very wrong if these promises and ostensible agreements are not delivered upon. Many expectations were created with all the stakeholders in order to get them to commit to processes and plans based on compromises by them all. Sipho realizes that the danger of this turning into a lose-lose situation is a real one—and he realizes the price of failure. He is aware of much frustration building up for all parties. He also realizes that he is in a position where he is expected to do something after receiving the phone call. Failing to act may compromise his position not only with the stakeholders but also with the potential employers on whom he depends to help him in job creation for the community. He cannot just leave things as they are and do nothing.

He is aware that the planning processes have been flawed. He knew it all along. Parties too quickly assumed that they understood each other. Differences were mostly underestimated. Many of the people merely focused on the gains they saw for themselves in the negotiated settlements they agreed upon while trying to ignore the costs to their interest positions. In this way they underestimated the overall perspective of the complex history and different interests of the other parties that always carried the potential for misunderstanding and conflict. The project decisions were in some cases based on tunnel vision and an attitude of let us just get this going! Harry, on several occasions, was one of the people who thought he knew it all and that he could gain control in a way that underestimated the complexities of the situation as well as the eventual costs for the interests of his constituency. Even during their telephone conversation Harry once again claimed he had all the information, but to Sipho it was evident that Harry and his constituency clearly had not thought through all the scenarios and the onerous "what if?" questions. Sipho is not optimistic, especially as he has to deal with people as narrow-minded as Harry, whose final and fast becoming only remedy was the old style reaction to bring in the police. He did not particularly like Harry or his approach to these issues.

Sipho considers his options. He could just do nothing and let things develop. Taking this option in the past sometimes helped, as the issues tended to ripen naturally and were handled as a matter of course during the already established forums and processes. Sipho realizes, however, that this time the issues are too complex and intense to leave to the established ways of dealing with them. Harry's adamancy confirms this, and the project is at such an advanced and crucial stage that doing nothing is not an option now.

Another option is to contribute to creating a crisis that would let the whole thing blow up. Sipho could go ahead and act in a way that would deliberately make things worse. If this approach leads to full scale disaster in the form of a bloody conflict, all parties would be forced to face the consequences, apply their minds anew, and either compromise through negotiations or live with a disastrous stalemate until they come to their senses. Sipho knows that this is sometimes the only option in a hard situation, where people have entrenched ideas and where they think that their interests will be served by being stubborn and recalcitrant. His experience during the liberation struggles taught him that under difficult circumstances this may the only way to go. He is also aware, though, that this approach can be very costly and destroy many valuable things and devastate whatever limited goodwill may have started to emerge between the involved parties. After some thought and consideration he decides that this is not the option to follow. At least not yet.

Sipho also accepts that he has some power and responsibility in this situation, but that his power is not going to give him enough influence to enforce a solution. At best it could help to use this limited power to assist in creating a process where all the stakeholders are brought together to reflect on the situation and its possible consequences and to come up with a negotiated solution. He senses that all stakeholders may just be able to realize that the gains that were hard won may exceed the possible losses to all parties through a decimating conflict. He therefore considers the third option, namely to use his influence in such a way that all concerned be brought back to a process where they are forced to face the current reality and its potential to destroy what has been achieved by many sacrifices and valuable compromises.

He therefore decides to plan for and work toward the implementation of a process to get all the stakeholders together to consider the nature of their current challenges. For this he would have to convince all the people in his circle of influence that they would have to join in the process and accept the responsibility and work that needs to be done to craft a new way ahead. He would also have to convince interest groups such as those represented by Harry to join in. As he has less influence over them, it may mean he might have to invoke the assistance of higher political and executive authorities if necessary. He has to contribute to successfully creating a space where all concerned could, with some feeling of safety, get together to work out a compromise and a new basis for action. He has to do this by means of a careful and considered strategy implemented with sensitivity, but also deliberately.

Sipho accepts that he does not have the power or authority to solve this problem on his own. However, if he could succeed in getting all the stakeholders involved in a process to seriously deal with the situation, which if not addressed could have serious consequences, he may just succeed in contributing to ward off a possible disaster. He would have to start making contact with relevant people immediately.

Adriaan Schout is an associate professor at the Open University in the Netherlands.

Case 8 Comments:
Reporting the Local News

What Is Wrong and What Should Be Done?

Steve Adubato

Clearly Victor is in a tough spot. Irynna is holding a lot of cards in a situation like this, but not all of them. The fact that Irynna is difficult and negative—and as Victor says, "a poor excuse for an editor"—is relevant but frankly shouldn't determine how Victor handles the situation. He needs to reframe the dialogue, elevate the discourse, and either bring in Irynna or isolate her as the obstructionist that she appears to be. This takes a variety of skills that few town managers or any individuals possess. We're talking skills of negotiation, leadership, conflict resolution, media skills, and the art of persuasion. All of these are about communication competence.

While there are no guarantees, Victor's best bet is to ask Irynna a few direct, but not overly confrontational, questions. He needs to see himself as more of a facilitator of a conversation. His objective is to engage those in the meeting, including Irynna. He has depersonalized the situation as much as possible between himself and the editor. When talking to Irynna, he needs to ask questions like "Irynna, what exactly are you looking for?" "How would you have handled this situation differently?" "What do you think most of the residents in our town really want from our government?" and "How can we work together in a more cooperative fashion in an effort to help our town . . . which is clearly what both of us want?"

Notice that much of the language revolves around "us" and "we." The subtle message is that we are all in this together, including Irynna, who may not want to see it that way. Victor needs to engage the others in the same fashion. He also needs to find ways to acknowledge points that are raised as meaningful contributions to the larger dialogue. This includes comments made by Irynna, as distasteful as that may be to Victor.

The communication techniques that Victor needs to employee really revolve around the art of facilitation, but they are also about public negotiation and achieving a positive outcome. Victor, or any other public manager/administrator who finds himself in this predicament, should set the tone for the conversation right up front. Make it clear exactly what he's attempting to accomplish. He needs to say it early and often so that there is no confusion. Great facilitators/negotiators are great listeners. They don't do a lot of talking and spend much of the time asking smart questions and concentrating on the answers. They also take their time responding to what they've heard as opposed to reacting in an unnecessarily adversarial fashion. Even if you don't like the other person or his communication style, you're negotiating because you have to. If you could simply get your way, you wouldn't be in this situation. Therefore, no matter how you feel about the other party, stay focused on the issues that need to be resolved. The key is to remember that communicating your distaste decreases the chance that you will accomplish your objectives. Simply put, focus more on the problem and less on the person.

Victor should try to communicate from Irynna's point of view. Great negotiators work hard to see the process as an opportunity to help someone else accomplish his or her objective.

If you go into a negotiation with a hard and fast definition of "winning" you are likely to be disappointed. And unless you are willing to walk away, this is a risky position to take.

Victor must be clear about what he wants, but he shouldn't dig his heels in too deep. It's important that he communicate his goals in the negotiation process while being flexible enough to respond to opportunities that present themselves in the process.

Whether you are a town manager like Victor or a government official who must persuade reluctant constituencies on a particular issue or initiative, it's all about connecting with others on a meaningful level. It's about empathizing and compromising. It's about having passion and being persistent while also being flexible. But in the final analysis it is all about being a superior communicator.

Steve Adubato, PhD, is a four-time Emmy Award–winning commentator with the PBS flagship station in New York, Channel Thirteen/WNET.

I. H. Meyer

In the Meeting

The town manager must engage in a meaningful dialogue with the editor and publisher of the newspaper first, even if he sees a deadlock on the horizon. My advice to the town manager is not to try to change the mind of the editor since it is apparent that the editor has already adopted a negative attitude. Instead, the manager should deal with the issues head-on. He should let Irynna know how disappointed he is with the newspaper's coverage of municipal functions, in particular her coverage of the citizen satisfaction survey. All the while, the town manager needs to maintain a level of professionalism and not allow the conversation to get personal. The town manager should avoid becoming defensive because this will aggravate the current situation. The town manager must effectively communicate his frustration and dissatisfaction with the negative press coverage and provide concrete examples of how this negative media attention has impacted service delivery. He should let the editor and publisher know that this type of coverage has a profound impact on the morale of the municipal staff and most certainly paints a negative picture of the township in the eyes of the reader.

During the meeting, the town manager should listen carefully to what Katherine and Irynna have to say. He should attempt to ascertain why they feel they must report things in such a negative light. Maybe they are feeling pressure to sell papers and to sell advertising space, and we all know that failures, and disasters, sell papers. People like to read about controversy; that's why tabloids sell. Together they should strive to come to an understanding of one another's perspectives. Hopefully, during this meeting the council representatives and university professors will have something constructive to add to the conversation.

After the Meeting

If the meeting does not lead to a favorable outcome, the town manager should write a series of guest columns for the newspaper that focus on the current projects of the municipality. The articles should paint a realistic picture of the township. To be taken as credible, the articles cannot read as blatant self-promotion or self-congratulatory remarks. The plan would be to run a series of such articles so residents gain insight into municipal operations and functions from the manager's perspective. One of the articles should focus exclusively on the results of the survey and the performance measurement initiative. The university professor could even write a column explaining the survey and the results in laymen's terms.

If the editor and publisher are opposed to the town manager writing a column for the paper, the manager could explore the possibility of publishing a *Municipal Gazette,* a free community newsletter, as an instrument to communicate with its citizens. The launch of the *Municipal Gazette* should not be introduced as competition to the *Petersburg Gazette,* but as the official mouthpiece of the municipality.

If all else fails, the manager could explore the possibility of creating the office of an independent media ombudsman to enable citizens and elected officials to lodge official complaints against the newspaper for inaccurate coverage. The town manager and elected officials must be willing to accept the outcome of the verdict of the media ombudsman even if the council and manager were to lose the case, as such a move would demonstrate the organizational and democratic maturity of the council.

My personal advice to the town manager is to adopt an attitude that the council and its citizens are bigger than he is and that he should focus on establishing civic participation and democratic morality as the building blocks of good local governance.

I. H. Meyer is the chief director of the Western Cape Provincial Administration, South Africa.

Susan C. Paddock

The only thing worse than not responding when attacked is responding in anger. When we're angry our ability to think clearly and logically may fly out the window. Thomas Jefferson once said, "When angry, count ten before you speak; if very angry, a hundred." The practitioners of the martial arts understand that controlling one's anger is essential in being able to overcome an aggressor.

Victor needs to control his anger . . . but this is just the first step. He *does* need to respond. Failure to respond suggests either that he is power-less in the face of Irynna or that he believes that she has a right to behave as she does. In responding, though, he must remember, to paraphrase Randolph Hearst, the danger of picking a fight with someone who buys ink by the barrel. He needs to choose how and where to respond.

Victor has done all one might normally do to foster good relations with the media. He has gone "above and beyond" to develop a working relationship with the newspaper, even when the paper's editorial approach became adversarial. Certainly a part of his anger is because he knows just how much he *has* done, and how patient he has been. Understanding his own emotions, and their basis, is being emotionally intelligent and is key to managerial success. So Victor needs to count to 10, or 100, and pay attention to those emotions, being sure that he understands and controls them rather than letting his emotions control the situation.

Victor should take another deep breath, count to 10 again, and con-sider why Irynna may be responding as she is. Is this what Irynna believes she needs to do for her career development? Does she think that trashing Petersburg will ensure her promotion? If this does not appear to be stan-dard procedure for the publisher, Victor will find that he is standing on firmer ground.

Having taken a deep breath or two and counted to 10 or 100, Victor might then ask Irynna, "What would it take to change your mind?" Reengaging Irynna in the discussion will let Katherine see how Irynna is framing her editorial policy. It may allow Katherine to see that Irynna is willing to act unethically, or is being unreasonable, and will let Victor see how Katherine responds to Irynna's policy. Is Katherine willing to rein in Irynna?

Katherine's response may not be any more satisfactory than Irynna's. She may find Irynna's obstinacy and unreasonableness acceptable. Then Victor needs to consider whether he should take the battle to a higher level.

What other media outlets serve Petersburg? What television or radio stations serve the area? These media can be used to counteract the newspaper's message. In doing so, Victor must remember that he may be exacerbating the situation. If he believes that this issue quickly will become part of everyday conversation in Petersburg's coffee shops, workplaces, and living rooms, then he should take his message to other media outlets, relying, perhaps, on the public information office of the university to make his case.

If, however, the issue is being discussed in only a few circles, Victor must understand that once he chooses to engage in battle, more of Petersburg's citizens, including those who never read a newspaper, will become involved in the issue. It will become increasingly difficult to separate fact from opinion. He may find himself found guilty of practicing good public administration, where, as cynics often note, "No good deed goes unpunished."

Whatever happens in the room that day, or in the newspaper in the ensuing days, Victor also must ensure that his working relationship with the university has not been damaged. Spending time with the professors who worked on this project, and giving a "heads up" to the university's public information office, will demonstrate an interest in having a strong and enduring relationship. It will make a powerful organization—the university—an ally.

Finally, Victor must remember that he is not alone in finding Irynna unreasonable and difficult. Naming the problem and finding agreement with others about the nature of the problem and how they will respond to it in a consistent manner will help Victor realize that he is not on his own. It will provide him with a sense of security so that, in the future, he may even be able to look back on this situation and laugh about it . . . not now, but someday.

Susan C. Paddock teaches public administration and directs the Certified Public Manager's Program at the University of Wisconsin.

Case 9 Comments:
Returning Home to Serve

What Is Wrong and What Should Be Done?

Valiant Clapper

Repatriates who have returned to "rescue" their colleagues with their newfound knowledge and worldly experience may be surprised that their colleagues oppose being "rescued." Kouakou faces the very real challenge of taking himself and his recently acquired knowledge too seriously. Solutions packaged in foreign countries may arouse chagrin and suspicion among those who have stayed home and have continuously worked at their country's problems. The challenge faced by Kouakou is how to utilize his "superior knowledge" with discernment and circumspection so as not to offend and possibly intimidate colleagues lacking formal training and education.

Kouakou has to come to terms with the fact that effective and efficient management and service delivery requires discernment that is not only other-regarding, but also self-effacing. Those who have worked hard in his country possess knowledge and skills that need to be acknowledged as well. His local image can only benefit from his recognition of indigenous habits, knowledge, and authority lines. It is necessary for Kouakou to focus on an inclusive approach to solutions, appreciating the potential worth and contribution of all the stakeholders.

The twin frustrations of nonacceptance and loneliness that Kouakou faces could conceivably be related to his evident inclination toward pursuing his own path to efficient service delivery, rather than acknowledging the prevailing departmental structures, hierarchies, organizational culture, and climate. The need to be culturally sensitive and accepting of existing patterns of operation and beliefs is something that should not have caught him off-guard, as it evidently did. In light of this, Kouakou should consider becoming a team player, and in so doing win some friends, influence some people, and ultimately benefit his work. He should pursue external funding, but in consultation with his coworkers. In this way Kouakou could become more of an organizational citizen as opposed to a lone decision-maker and sole executive suspicious of the capabilities of his colleagues. He would become more respectful of his new work environment and of the indigenous knowledge systems and habits.

Valiant Clapper is a research professor at Tshwane University of Technology in Pretoria, South Africa.

Robert Cunningham

The main elements of this case ring true—the shortage of resources, the jealousy of peers and subordinates, suspicion by the superior, the requests/demands of clients. One unmentioned element that one may also suspect will increase the pressure on Kouakou is the expectation of relatives and friends for special treatment—whether this is access to resources over which he has control, or requests for help in obtaining government employment or resources from other government departments.

I suspect that the resource shortage problem cannot be solved. The case author is correct that attempting to get funds from outside sources will elevate feelings of jealousy and may reduce the government contribution to his budget. (We do that in the United States when a "sales tax increase for education" passes the legislature, and then other sources of education revenue are reduced.)

Creating a central database does not strike me as a priority. There are multiple ways to sabotage a system, and with more enemies than friends, Kouakou will become an easy target. He should concentrate on building human relationships across the gamut of stakeholders in his city.

Kouakou must become political—not in an ideological way, but in a relational way. He should do a personal ethics inventory to sort out his value system and decide where he is willing to compromise and where he will be unwilling to compromise. It would be helpful for him to talk to older people whom he trusts and respects in helping him develop an ethical position. Once he has sorted himself out, he must get to know people, starting with those older people to whom he has connections, and ask them to introduce him to people they respect. Kouakou must develop a network. He must do favors for others and ask others to do favors for him.

He should not be secretive, but he should keep a low profile. Visibility attracts jealousy and a desire of others to pull you down. Use the influence one accumulates to further one's social goals, not one's personal position. Justify changes in the name of maintaining traditional values, which is not usually hard to do.

Kouakou needs a highly placed protector because if he is effective in accomplishing even small changes, he will develop enemies. Repay a protector by supplying him with useful information. Information and doing favors are your assets. Keep your eyes and ears open.

Come to work early, work hard, befriend subordinates—they will be glad to help you. Develop a reputation for honesty and discretion. Provide reasonable help whenever you can. Read and apply *Getting to Yes*.

The problem situation described above has no short-run solution. Even attempting to follow the principles indicated here, Kouakou may experience a number of defeats before tasting success. The situation is like learning to play soccer or badminton: You can read the rulebook, but that won't do much for teaching you the game; you have to practice, analyze your performance, correct your mistakes, and try again. High-level performance requires practice, and winning is never guaranteed.

Robert Cunningham researched, studied, and taught in the Middle East for 6 years. Currently he teaches public administration at the University of Tennessee.

Andi Zhamierashvili

Kouakou's key problem is his shrinking budget. But this is a typical problem of any developing country, where the public sector services leave much to be desired, the economy is not developed, and the agricultural sector is struggling to survive. Returning home from France, Kouakou knew he would have budget problems when he accepted the job of director of social services in West Africa. His second challenge is how to achieve more with less—that is, respond to all requests in a timely manner and try to accommodate most requests for assistance. The third problem, the absence of a proper filing system, Kouakou has already solved by creating a filing department and putting one of his staff members in charge of it. However, there are no funds to put the client information service on-line. In addition, an underlying tension exists between Kouakou, the young, college-educated repatriate who has new ideas on how things could be done, and the older generation of employees, who lack formal education but possess intimate knowledge of the community and community needs. Last, but not the least challenge for Kouakou, is to not get discouraged and not to look for other jobs.

Because Kouakou faces financial and understaffing problems he should ensure that the department is getting the most out of the staff they have and should look into ways of increasing productivity, perhaps through a system of rewards for hard-working staff. Given that Kouakou's numerous requests to receive more government funds for his department have ended in fiasco, he has the option of developing a new project proposal where he will outline the whole *raison-d'etre* for the Department of Social Services. Kouakou is full of good will. He genuinely wants to achieve improvements in his field and make a difference in the public sector. His determination could help him to receive some external funding for his office. If successful, he could even put the client information service on-line, as he originally planned. However, external funds can only last for a few years. What happens when the funding is over? By that time, if the government funding is still small, Kouakou could introduce a minimum fee-based service to keep Social Services running.

However, all of the above will be possible only if Kouakou has a united team that is willing to implement necessary changes in the way the department delivers its services. It will not be easy to convince his old-fashioned employees that there could be more efficient ways of doing business and that continuing to do "business as usual" is wrong. He needs to have his staff on his side, not against him when implementing the changes he has in mind. Therefore, he should use all his diplomatic skills to get their full support. There is nothing more counterproductive than having staff, or colleagues, who instead of helping in the implementation of the work plan, block it every step of the way.

In conclusion, Kouakou needs to apply his "know how," gained in France, to maximize his current financial and human resources for the benefit of the public. He needs to recognize the value of his colleagues and acknowledge their contributions to the process. In no way should he act superior to the people he works with. It is obvious they are a bit distrusting and suspicious. Kouakou needs to do everything within his power to build trust and earn their trust. While working on this, Kouakou should continue his efforts to secure funding from foreign donors as an option, which will allow him to increase the level of service offered. An increase in efficiency of Social Services may in the long term attract additional public funds for his department.

Andi Zhamierashvili, a native of the Republic of Georgia, works for the Food and Agriculture Organization of the United Nations in Rome, Italy.

Case 10 Comments:
Computer Problems at the Library

What Is Wrong and What Should Be Done?

Jonathan Justice

"Get on with it."

The problem here may be mainly that the library system's director does not have enough confidence in himself and his remaining available resources. He needs to get a grip and avoid panicking, so that he can get on with the work that needs to be done to get the new system up and running and deal with the loss of a key manager. If he has come to depend very heavily on the assistant director alone among his managers, it is understandable that he is momentarily at a loss. Facing a hiring freeze with a fully utilized staff may appear daunting as well. Still, it is unlikely that a replacement assistant director could have been recruited and installed quickly enough for that to have been a solution, even without the hiring freeze. Abandoning or delaying the new system's implementation until available staff can get suitable training and experience—or until the hiring freeze is lifted and a replacement assistant director hired—is always an option should worst come to worst, but is probably not necessary. In fact, I would urge the director to continue with the implementation schedule, making use of available knowledge and human resources from within and around the library to manage the project.

This means that there is a great deal to be done. First, the resigning assistant director needs to document her knowledge of the project and her dealings with the vendor by preparing a comprehensive project progress and status report and briefing the director, the implementation committee, and the new project manager on status and significant issues. Assuming the separation is a cordial one, she should be perfectly happy to do this, and it should be possible for the new project manager to follow up with her for specific questions as they arise later.

Next, it seems likely that among the remaining 24 employees of the library there is likely to be at least one with some level of suitable aptitude and interest. Presumably the most technical aspects of data conversion, software adaptation, and staff training are to be performed by the vendor, so the task is mainly one of project management rather than programming or technical training. The director should not be too quick to eliminate the three support-staff members on the implementation committee from initial consideration. There may be talent and interest there, unbeknownst to the director. Regardless of whom the director designates as project manager, that person will need at least from time to time to rely on the director's backing and expressions of urgency to get cooperation from others. Project management in organizations often relies more on persuasion and moral authority, supplemented by expressions of interest from top executives, than on the project managers' position-derived authority.

And the director *will* have to make clear to himself and others that this project is a top priority for the few months it will take to implement. That means that some routine operations may have to suffer and that there may be some delays in processing the acquisition of new research materials or other activities for a few weeks while the project is implemented. Individual and business library patrons are entitled to fair warning and an explanation that the exigencies of getting the new system installed and operating well require some temporary inconvenience, as are library staffers.

Also, the director should not discount the possibility that donated expertise may be available among library patrons, too—once the situation is explained, it may be possible to recruit volunteer experts to the implementation committee from outside the library staff. Additional help may also be available from the regional government, which will want to protect its $300,000 investment and avoid appearing to voters to have wasted the money now that its executive has signed the contract.

Finally, the director needs to remind himself and other stakeholders that significant organizational projects are almost always disruptive. They typically involve temporary reallocations of resources away from organizational slack or routine functions, and when they involve wholesale system changes (whether computer systems or human-administrative systems) they are particularly challenging. Let the director take courage: Compared to the other challenges and inconveniences we would normally expect to be associated with a project such as this one, the loss of a key manager is pretty minor.

Jonathan Justice teaches public administration at the University of Delaware.

Gail Kenny

One of the nicest things about working in a governmental or university setting is the insularity of the environment. Everyone tends to know everyone else, and it is unwise to develop a reputation for leaving responsible and challenging tasks undone. So it is in the best interests of the director, the recently departed assistant director, and the director of projects and grants to pull together in an effort to successfully implement the new system. In fact, that becomes the priority because any deterioration of day-to-day service under the old system will be quickly forgotten once the new one is in place.

The library is really only losing one management position, and since no one will be hired as a replacement, all of the assistant director's responsibilities will be divided among the remaining staff anyway, including this implementation.

Ideally the assistant director left a written schedule. Follow it. Review the minutes of the implementation committee. Normally software vendors are dying to help make their product soar. Use the money saved from the resignation to buy vendor expertise, sign the library director and projects director up for as many technical training classes as can be found, and entice the former employee to contribute as a consultant (ideally, most of the exit interview was devoted to this topic). You may not have the in-house expertise on March 31, but there is no excuse not to have more of it by May 31.

Finally, assess the talents in the implementation committee. It is quite possible that among that group, there is an individual capable of stepping into place to oversee the process.

Gail Kenny is the finance director for Oreland, Pennsylvania.

Sarmistha Rina Majumdar

The main problem seems to be the poor management decision of the director of the regional library. As seen in this case, he fails to provide the much needed guidance and direction in the overhauling process of the library's computer system. He makes the mistake of assigning the entire responsibility to the assistant director, who is responsible for the maintenance of the library's computer system. This reflects bad judgment on his part—to rely on a single person in executing such a massive project that involves several steps.

In delegation of responsibilities to a single person without any support staff to assist her, we find evidence of the director's underestimation of the tediousness of the task. This partly helps to explain why he thought it was unnecessary to organize a team from among his managerial and professional staff. It could have helped to ease the process of transition to the new computer technology with the least friction.

The assistant director was entrusted with the massive task of organizing and implementing changes in the library's computer system. In addition to her regular duties, she had to oversee the whole process of selection of a new computer system, contract negotiation, training, implementation, and contract management. No doubt she was overburdened with work. In an effort to reduce her workload, she formed an implementation committee composed of staff members. Despite that, she decided to resign. Under such circumstances, it may not be wrong to speculate that she resigned under the intense pressure of work. Her resignation was in protest to the director's unfair allocation of responsibilities.

Also, in delegation of the entire responsibility to the assistant director, we find that the director made the classic mistake of putting all the eggs in one basket. He not only over-relied on a single person to execute the task but had also failed to contemplate the consequences of sudden resignation of that employee. Undoubtedly, it was the director's poor management decision that led to a crisis situation in the library.

The director of the regional library needs to make greater use of his leadership skills and play a more proactive role in the overhauling process of the library's computer system. In view of the several steps involved in adoption of the new technology in the library and the fact that every staff member is going to benefit from it, he ought to involve them in every step of the project. So he should form a team and delegate the task to it rather than to a single employee.

The director's responsibility should not end with the formation of the team. Neither should he isolate himself from the team at any stage of the project. As the leader of the team, he should provide constant guidance and direction throughout the course of the project. It is equally important for him to oversee and coordinate the activities of team members. This can help avoid the complexity that often arises from joint action among members from various subdivisions/departments.

In a teamwork approach, he can utilize the expertise of both managerial and professional staff members in the organization and implementation of the project. If every team member is assigned the job for which he or she is best suited, there is a greater possibility of that job being done efficiently and with the least friction. Also, it would lead to greater cooperation among staff members.

Further, the involvement of various staff members in the project can help to eliminate the problem of over-reliance on a single person. With the delegation of responsibilities among several members, none of them will feel overburdened with work. Neither will it raise the issue of unfair allocation of responsibilities in the workplace. Also, if any team member decides to quit his or her job while working on the project, its impact will be minimal. The project will not come to an unexpected halt and create a crisis situation.

At the end of the project, the director should not fail to acknowledge the contribution of team members. He should attribute the success of the project to them. This would help to make their participation worthwhile and leave them with a sense of pride and accomplishment.

Sarmistha Rina Majumdar, a native of India, teaches public administration at the University of North Texas.

Case 11 Comments: Getting Support for Good Works

What Is Wrong and What Should Be Done?

Koen M. Becking

The problem is of a twofold nature. On the one hand, the main character lacks insight into the cultural habits in Russia. On the other hand, she lacks managerial, organizational, and communicative skills.

The problem is, of course, complex. The international arena is not easy to understand. The most difficult aspect is culture; it is hard to get a true understanding of what is really going on in a country. This is underlined by the fact that communication is also very difficult. English is primarily used as the international language, but not all participants and parties involved are equally skilled at communicating in English. Nuance is frequently lost.

Another clear problem is the vast number of organizations (including nongovernmental organizations) and donors working abroad. The intentions of all these organizations are not the same. Large organizations, such as the UN or World Bank, have different priorities and goals than the local people and organizations.

It appears that Melanie is a little naive and overenthusiastic about the possible outcomes of the work she does (i.e., organizing a conference). For example, when there is no response from two powerful AIDS players in the republic—the local UN representatives and the Republican AIDS Center— she moves on with her own work. At this stage it would be preferable to get into contact with these organizations—not only to establish an understanding of what she is doing, but to network and to make sure things are done effectively and not duplicated numerous times by different organizations. The only way to establish sustainable relations is by meeting these people.

So Melanie better get out there and make sure there is support from both the UN and the local organizations. Melanie must be persistent and insistent upon meeting all the stakeholders to better serve her constituents.

This is exactly where the biggest problem arises. The preparation in terms of meetings, coordination, and planning was not sufficient. When Melanie finally met representatives of both the UN and the Republican AIDS Center, she did not have a chance.

Melanie was already set back by a lack of good communication in the first stages of her activities. She encountered even more problems when meeting the chief doctor after she went to the UN representatives. She entered into disputes and arguments she should have stayed out of. The invitation to attend the National Conference therefore was no more than a respectful way for them to be decent and make clear that next time she could do better.

When Melanie finally decides to talk to the executive director, there is little left that she can do for this project other than start again and try not to make the same mistakes. She should try to get the funds for the same project another time or another project another time. Also, I think she makes the same mistake with her executive director as she did with the project. She contacts him at a stage where things are irreversible. Communication in an earlier stage may have been more fruitful and she could have used the authority and expertise of her boss as she might have used the experience and authority of UN officials and local representatives of the Republican AIDS Center.

Koen M. Becking is the executive director of the Dutch Public Sector Training Institute in the Netherlands.

Peter F. Haruna

Although this case study focuses our attention on an HIV training seminar in the former Soviet Union, it can be generalized to other sectors and regions to enhance understanding of cross-cultural and international cooperation. The case exemplifies an administrative mindset that aid workers and development practitioners need to confront, one that is based on narrow rational thought and that, in the long run, proves to be ineffective, as this analysis intends to argue.

When a development program hits a wall or runs into difficulties, it is tempting to take the people-blaming approach by framing the problem in terms of individual characteristics, emphasizing mean attitudes, abrasive personalities, incompetence, or even neurotic tendencies of some people. In this case study, Dr. Georgy Apaguni and the two UN officials may be blamed for taking an aggressive, uncooperative position. Likewise, Melanie Geans may be blamed for incompetence, and Volodya and Irina for untrustworthiness. However, while pinpointing individuals for blame might explain the cause of the difficulties, this provides a simplistic explanation and blocks the possibility of seeing the problem in a comprehensive fashion.

It is equally tempting to explain the delay of the HIV training seminar in terms of the dysfunctional bureaucracy, particularly the inflexibility in adhering to the "national AIDS treatment protocol." In fact, the local partners in Belogorsk expressed that much, referring to "a bunch of bureaucrats acting all important in the capital." Of course, bureaucrat bashing is justified if rules are both confusing and excessive and if employees behave unreasonably rather than prudently. Nonetheless, this approach is highly limited and may result in frustration when confronted with intractable and apparent irrational forces such as the widespread "informal networks" existing in the former Soviet Union.

While these two approaches may differ, they share a common theme in rational thought, as when Medicines to People wrote letters and sent faxes and e-mails. They point to important phenomena in implementing development programs, but they are incomplete and oversimplified. How then can the problem be fruitfully reframed in a manner that opens a window to the reality of development administration both in the former Soviet Union and other regions of the world?

In contrast to the restrictive approaches, it is possible to see the problem more holistically based on a critical, pragmatic, and multidisciplinary perspective, one that embraces historical legacies; social, cultural, and economic conditions; political regime restrictions; and organizational limitations. In other words, the unique circumstances of the former Soviet Union should not be ignored but rather require a more complex lens for explaining and addressing problems of public concern such as the HIV/AIDS epidemic in the region.

Having emerged from nearly a century of authoritarian rule with a highly centralized and overbearing bureaucracy, the former Soviet Union should not be expected to change overnight despite reform efforts since 1989. This historical legacy might partially explain why people from the capital are inclined to "control the HIV agenda" and why the Republican AIDS Center based in the capital is powerful. A single-minded pursuit of narrowly conceptualized rationality is inadequate or even disastrous in the long run. Cross-cultural cooperation must expand the conception of rationality by considering the unique circumstances of different societies.

If this analysis is correct, Melanie will need to do at least three things. First, she has to meet with her sponsors immediately to explain and make the case for rescheduling the training seminar. Second, she has to personally contact and establish a working relationship with all major actors on the ground. Finally, she needs to study and factor in the socio-cultural conditions reflected in years of "informal networks" into the design of any future training seminars.

Peter F. Haruna is an assistant professor of public administration and MPA program coordinator at Texas A&M International University in Laredo, Texas. He is originally from Ghana (West Africa), where he worked in different capacities for both government and nongovernmental agencies.

Jyl Josephson

The problem presented by this case is not nearly as great as Melanie Geans fears. However, the case provides important lessons both for working on local development projects with community partners and for managing funding relationships.

Issue #1: Implementing
Effective Local Development Projects

The literature on community development shows very clearly that it is crucial to the success of any project to include local partners in the planning process. Much of the critique of, for example, United Nations development projects of the 1960s and 1970s was due to the fact that these projects were often planned with no knowledge of local conditions. Rather, a template was developed that was then applied to many different contexts, often with limited or negative effects.

This project was planned to include participation of local contacts, but this seems to be the weakest part of the implementation of the project. Given the difficulty of the local/national partnership and the need to maintain positive relationships with the national partner, it would seem that in the future, Medicines to People may wish to build in more time for developing these relationships. After all, designing a project that responds to the needs of those who will be carrying on the long-term work of HIV/AIDS prevention will be the only way to make effective use of the grantor's funds.

Another important point from the perspective of the literature on community development is that successful work of this kind requires looking at the already existing assets in a community. Assets take many forms, and the people assets of a community are crucial to project success. Melanie Geans seems to be viewing the local contact, Irina, as an asset, while she seems to be viewing Dr. Georgy Apaguni, the director of the AIDS Center, as a problem. Turning this around, and seeing this government official as an asset, would help her see the problems and issues differently. This official, even if his manner is difficult, even if he is protecting his turf, is an important asset. After all, he has access to resources and influence. Cultivating the relationship with this official might help in cultivating relationships with the other local agencies that had other priorities and chose not to host the training activities that Medicines to People had planned.

Issue #2: Maintaining the Grantor/Grantee Relationship

Melanie seems to be very concerned about the reputation of her organization, particularly in relation to her grant-giving agency. But the reputation of Medicines to People was not developed through only one project and it is not going to fall on this one project. Nevertheless, there are things that Melanie could have done, and could now do, to make sure that this relationship and the reputation of her organization remain intact.

First, the case notes that the grantor verbally approved the changes, but it would be more prudent to have a document trail. Depending upon the specifics of the grant agreement, Melanie should have prepared a set of proposed changes to the grant and submitted these to the grantor in writing. This would provide for a clearer record of accountability regarding the grant.

Second, the goal of Melanie's organization and of the grant-giving organization is the same: to make effective use of the available funds to improve HIV/AIDS education and outreach in the former Soviet Union. Sometimes effective use does not correspond either to grant funding cycles or to the format laid out in the grant proposal. Thus, Melanie should consider at this point whether it is possible to renegotiate the grant. Medicines for People can show that it has begun to develop relationships of trust with local parties. It can also show that trying to continue with the original plan in terms of the end date of the grant would be contrary to the goals of both the funding organization and Medicines to People. Especially if the costs of the grant have been less than initially planned (given the reduction in training sites and days), Melanie should request an extension of the monies to the next funding cycle, using the remaining grant money to run a second workshop and maintain the local relationships.

Jyl Josephson is the director of women's studies at Rutgers University–Campus at Newark.

Case 12 Comments: An Office Romance

What Is Wrong and What Should Be Done?

Alma Joseph

Mary must realize that she is key to the investigation. Although she may not know how and when the inappropriate behavior began, she has some knowledge of the situation as it existed more than 6 years ago.

There is nothing in the scenario that would indicate that Bill made unwanted advances to Claudette. In fact, according to the information presented, Claudette appeared to be the aggressor during the lunch. It was Bill who appeared to be surprised by Claudette's actions. Nevertheless, if Claudette was telling the truth at the time, there was inappropriate behavior by Bill. As a supervisory officer at the institution, he was in a position of power and therefore he is held to a higher standard. Bill is responsible for ensuring that his actions cannot be misinterpreted—that is, his actions should be beyond reproach.

There was a time when an individual had to make it known that the comments, or advances, were unwanted, and if the behavior persisted, the individual could file a claim of sexual harassment. Rejection of unwanted behavior is no longer a requirement; a claim can be filed after the first unwanted comment or inappropriate behavior. In addition, claims of harassment can arise from third parties who believe that they have been adversely affected by the relationship between others in the workplace. Thus, if Claudette felt that she had to "play footsies" with Bill in order to compete for promotional opportunities or if she felt that someone else was advancing because of an affair, then by definition, she would have a case of sexual harassment. Again, there are no details regarding the basis for the sexual harassment claim.

It does not appear that Mary has any information that would be damaging to Bill. Claudette's comment that she thought that Bill was in love with her would require additional corroborating information. Withholding this information and having it revealed later would do more damage to Mary's credibility and subsequently her career than coming forward at this time.

The investigator should address Mary's concern about her career. It would be unrealistic to expect that Mary would not be concerned about the impact on her career; however, this cannot be the determining factor for her. Retaliation against Mary for coming forward and telling the truth would be unlawful although understandably difficult to prove. Since it is clear that Mary is on Bill's team, it is unlikely that she would be part of the inner circle of an opposition candidate.

Mary cannot avoid answering the questions that these allegations have raised.

Alma Joseph is the assistant commissioner for human resources at the New Jersey Department of Human Services. She oversees the Office of Personnel Services, the Office of Cooperative Labor Relations, the Office of Human Resources Operational Excellence, and the Office of Equal Employment Opportunity and Affirmative Action.

Changhwan Mo

Although Mary's reluctance to participate in the investigation of Bill is understandable, nonetheless she must cooperate and tell the truth about what she observed several years ago. Moreover, she should clearly say that she did not influence Juanita's findings in the earlier case brought against Bill. Although Mary is scared that her participation could come back to haunt her, she has no option right now since the investigation is going to be made public anyway. Even if a political motive is behind this sexual harassment case, Mary still cannot avoid the investigation.

The representatives from the attorney general's office certainly have talked to several people who are close to Mary, so there is no doubt that she is now firmly in the middle of this investigation. She should fully cooperate with the investigation but continually maintain that she has in no way acted unethically. If she does not cooperate with the investigation, others may strongly suspect that she has something to hide.

Although Mary assumes that Bill did not sexually harass Claudette, the investigation may find evidence that sexual harassment had actually occurred. Since she does not know exactly what happened between Bill and Claudette, she should sincerely cooperate with the investigation. That is the best policy for her at this time.

Changhwan Mo is a research fellow with the Korea Transport Institute, South Korea.

Meredith Newman

What Is the Problem?

There are at least four problems. First, sexual harassment can take both overt and subtle forms. This particular case is illustrative of the latter and recounts the difficulties surrounding allegations of sexual harassment both in terms of the behavior itself and in determining the legitimacy of a claim of sexual harassment. Second, the case underscores the longevity of an accusation of sexual harassment. Even a claim that is formally found to be without merit can resurface years later, with potentially devastating consequences for all parties. Third, the case shines a bright light on the problem of office romances—in this case, between an older male supervisor and a much younger female subordinate. The relationship between Bill and Claudette seemingly began with "flirting" on the part of Claudette toward Bill. Parenthetically, whether Claudette herself is guilty of sexually harassing Bill depends upon the extent to which her behavior was welcome and invited. In any event, any office romance can be explosive if and when the relationship sours. Finally, there is the problem of perception. Whether or not Bill was guilty of sexual harassment, the mere hint of such behavior may be sufficient to derail his quest to become the next president of this large public university.

What Ought the Main Character Do?

Four things: First, seeking legal counsel is an appropriate and wise course of action. Mary's professionalism and reputation are at risk. Second, Mary should stay the course with her original assessment of the situation. She should not second-guess the formal assessment of a claim ruled on some 10 years prior, even with new allegations surfacing, namely a second-hand claim by a friend of Claudette's who said that Claudette told her that Bill had sexually harassed her in the past. Third, she should communicate her stance to Bill, Juanita, and Claudette. In her conversation with Claudette, Mary should inquire into the claim and weigh any revelations carefully. The fact that Claudette is now married and that she has left the state to avoid the investigation may be significant. Fourth, Mary should then have her lawyer communicate her position to the attorney general's office. If she truly believes that the claims of sexual harassment are unfounded and indeed driven by spurious motives, she should not personally engage with the attorney general's office unless legally required to do so. In any event, whether as a key witness or as a colleague and friend, Mary should hold fast to her beliefs. To do so

- supports the earlier findings of the formal investigation by Juanita,
- is consistent with her own interpretation of the earlier incident, and
- is the ethically sound thing to do.

To not do so

- would undermine the legitimacy of Juanita and her office and suggest that a minority woman cannot be trusted to rule objectively in a matter of importance;
- would erode her long-term relationship with Bill, who, it should be remembered, has already been judged to be not guilty of sexual harassment;
- would potentially cloud her own career and credibility in any attempt to second-guess what may or may not have occurred some 10 years prior (or in the intervening years, of which she has no first-hand knowledge); and
- would fundamentally be contrary to her original and subsequent opinion on the issue.

Meredith Newman, a native of Australia, teaches public administration at the University of Illinois, Springfield.

Case 13 Comments:
Moving Up in the Organization

What Is Wrong and What Should Be Done?

Janet Foley Orosz

Nick is a good judge of talent and created an environment in which hard-working, bright Mike could advance in the organization as he completed his education in public administration and established his career interests. Nick is well suited to help Mike evaluate his present situation in the Stores and Provisions Department. Nick has already spent 14 years in a mentoring relationship with Mike, advocating for the changes Mike worked on and for Mike's promotions. It's time for Mike to conduct his own situational assessment of his current employment and career situation—in essence it is time for Mike to treat his circumstance as a case study. (It's that theory-practice opportunity!)

Nick should meet several times with Mike and

1. Ask Mike to quickly construct and bring back an abbreviated situational assessment of the Stores and Provisions Department (Mike loved the strategic management course in his MPA program). Mike could, for example, spend a morning completing a SWOT (strengths, weaknesses, opportunities, threats) analysis of the organization, listing external events and trends affecting the department and strategic directions for the department of stores and provisions.

Among other things, the SWOT analysis would reveal Mike's view (and also Nick's) of the Stores and Provisions Department as a stable organization with a culture of employees of career-length tenure and low turnover. Yet within that structure, Nick maintained an organizational environment that provided career development opportunities (and rising pay) for Mike.

We are not told of the larger organizational context in which the Stores and Provisions Department sits. Is it a large or small general purpose government agency (city, state or department, or national level)? Are there other departments within the larger organization? We don't know the contextual environment of the larger organization, either. Is it an environment of tight budgets? The situational assessment process will cast a wider lens on Mike's career opportunities. Nick could ask if the horizon for career expansion can be expanded to the larger organization. What other opportunities could be considered?

2. Then Nick should ask Mike to conduct a situational assessment of Mike's own experiences as he moved up in the Stores and Provisions Department. Specifically, Mike should address the reasons for his successes when he used his developing skills

- on useful projects (of smaller scope),
- to streamline processes,
- to conduct an internal audit that led to eliminating unnecessary duplication, and
- to revise and analyze the existing departmental policies (applauded by superiors).

Mike could answer these questions about his success:

- What organizational conditions were needed and what conditions did Nick or others create for each project to be successful?
- What style and skill sets were necessary for each project to succeed and have the supportive climate to be implemented, successful, and rewarded?
- Who gave the okay for the projects developed by Mike, and who was involved in the decision to advance Nick along the way? In what environment and under what constraints do those individuals operate?
- What was the chain of command at each of these levels? What has changed during this time in the departmental environment?
- What type of change was Mike proposing after he reached the position of senior administrative officer (organizational restructuring and the development of a staff appraisal system)? What conditions were different? What was different about this set of changes that caused the chief director to intervene and choose another option?

Once Mike thinks about the situation as if it were a case study from his MPA program, he will have a broader view of his situation. His next step is to identify his options: (a) Stay in the organization and find other motivational/skill development outlets such as training, new responsibilities, or strategies to improve or establish a relationship with the current director in Stores and Provisions; (b) move to a job in the larger organization; or (c) take the teaching (or other) job. Nick will have dealt in a positive way with Mike's lowered morale.

Janet Foley Orosz teaches organizational theory at the University of Akron and facilitates the development of online courses in public administration for several degree programs in the United States.

Yusuf Sayed

The case study brings into play the interrelationships among the key actors who occupy different positions in the organizational hierarchy. There is Nick who is a long-serving member of the company, who became director after 31 years. Mike is a young, bright, and ambitious member who within a short space of time, through initiative and effort, became assistant director. There is also the chief director who resisted Mike's ideas.

In identifying what can be done, it is important to identify what the problem is. Clearly the immediate problem is Mike's sense of frustration at not being listened to and consequently his applying for—and being offered—another post. But such a post is different from his current job, and moreover the post that he has been offered is different from what he has done.

Nick feels that he has reached a position in the company that he is content with. He clearly feels that Mike is someone he can rely on, and more importantly, he has been a key asset to Nick in his position as deputy director. The chief director is less involved with Mike and indicates that he does not value highly, as Nick does, Mike's advice.

The situation has reached an impasse, and it is clear that the resolution of the situation depends on Nick's actions. Yet Nick seems unable to respond effectively to the situation.

Part of the explanation for this is that Nick does not wish to rock the boat. He has seemingly a static view of his career, in which progression depends on length of time and not offending senior staff. Yet at the same time he is able to recognize initiative, drive, and motivation. Moreover, Nick is very recent in his position as director and sees himself occupying the position of chief director in a year's time, given that the current incumbent is soon to retire. However, the key mistake Nick could make is that by not acting decisively and allowing his own views to be heard he may rule himself out of the position he desires. Thus, it is clear that Nick needs to act. Failure to do so would not only result in his losing a key ally and valued member, Mike, but would also mean that he is not seen as a senior manager who is able to act decisively.

It is clear that to date, Nick's attempt to support Mike has not met with much success. What Nick needs to do is to assert his views and ensure that the chief director listens to him. The problem is not just that the chief director is ignoring Mike but also that he is not listening to Nick. Nick clearly needs to ensure that he is heard and listened to by the chief director. Not acting and not stating his view is resulting in unnecessary stress to

Mike, who feels that he is being made to choose between the current position he enjoys and the teaching position at the technical training school. Nick needs to adjust his perspective so that he is seen as being able to stand up for his own views.

It is also evident that Mike is experiencing a high level of frustration and that his productivity is declining. Nick needs to be more supportive of Mike and coach him to accept that not all of his ideas will be accepted. While it is important that Mike's ideas be listened to, it is not the case that they all should be adopted. While the chief director may not have given Mike's idea full consideration, it is sensible to hire outside consultants for the task.

In this regard, Mike is in need of support and needs to be coached to accept disappointment and frustration. He needs to learn that opting out is not the only or the most preferable option. Clearly Nick needs to reassure Mike of his value to the company and that he has much to learn as well as offer to the company.

What is also clear is that the organizational structure of the company is unable to respond to those displaying initiative on a fast track advancement program. The organization needs to adjust to make this possible. Moreover, since it is clear that Mike will not be able to advance in the immediate future, there is a need to create a structure and work that keeps determined and bright staff motivated. To this end, Nick could also consider ways in which he can reward Mike and feed his motivation.

In all of this it is evident that perspective needs adjustment: Mike's single focus, the chief director's knee-jerk reaction to Mike's response to his frustration, and Nick's sense of powerlessness from being in the middle. Nick needs to recover his sense of agency, the chief director needs to listen more to young staff, and Mike needs to find ways of coping with setback without running.

In all of this, communication is the key. Communication is a two-way process involving both talking and listening. And it is evident that all three members do not talk to each other enough; nor do they listen well. Reacting by avoidance (Nick), by rejection (chief director), and by running (Mike) do not suggest an open organizational culture that is able to listen to all and allow grievances to be dealt with constructively. In the end, all three would be losers if the situation is not resolved; Nick will lose a valuable member of his staff, Mike will seek work that he does not find satisfactory, and the chief director will not have access to valuable insight and advice that is of benefit to the company.

Yusuf Sayed, PhD, is senior education advisor and education team leader for the Division on Foreign and International Development in the UK.

Naomi Wish

Times are changing. Right from the start, one reads that this problem is related to the age of the actors or stakeholders in the case.

Nick Brown, the director, is 49 years old and has the mindset of a 49-year-old employee. He has stayed with the same company for 31 years, even though "his advancement has been slow." He is content to end his career as director rather than chief director.

Mike, on the other hand, is 32 years old and has the mindset of a 32-year-old employee. His focus is on his own skills and career. He knows that he cannot count on one company giving him "a job for life" and probably wouldn't want that. He has demonstrated that he is a change agent, both for himself and his employer. He went back to school to continue his education while working full time and tried to bring his new skills and knowledge back to help his organization change and grow. Therefore, one would expect him to want to continue to make career moves, by changing employers as well as even changing careers.

Nick Brown has the problem because he has relied on Mike for 14 years. The case states, "Nick really did not want to see Mike leave—he was such a star performer—and he suspected that Mike didn't really want to leave, either." The word "suspected" is the key here. The first thing that Nick should do is meet with Mike to determine correctly the reasons Mike is not only leaving, but making a career move to academia. If Nick determines that Mike has always wanted a teaching career and that's the reason he pursued more higher education, he should wish him well and understand that if Mike stayed with the company, instead of taking the job he wanted, Mike probably would not be as effective as he had previously been.

However, if, after speaking with Mike, Nick determined that Mike wanted to stay with the company but was concerned that he wouldn't be promoted quickly enough, Nick could discuss the problem with the chief director and try to develop a career plan for Mike with annual goals and objectives that would be agreed upon by all three.

However, looking at the ages of Nick and Mike and their past behavior suggests it is very unlikely that Mike would really want to stay with the company under any circumstances. Times are changing, and Mike recognizes that and knows that he must keep moving—that is, developing his own skills and knowledge.

Naomi Wish is a professor and chair of the public administration program at Seton Hall University in South Orange, New Jersey.

Case 14 Comments: Training Grant Decisions

What Is Wrong and What Should Be Done?

Hedy Isaacs

This is a classic example of the extent to which dynamic organizational environments may influence agency policy and provide impulses for reappraisal of an agency's goals, leading to changes in organizational structures and strategies. It has been argued that when managers recognize the significance of their complex and uncertain environments and incorporate these in their decision making, they are more likely to satisfy the constituencies that they are set up to serve and achieve their agencies' goals. Managers are required to monitor changes in the environment and take action accordingly.

Jim Corliss, as the manager of the government agency responsible for the issue of training grants and the administrator for the Workforce Development Partnership Program (WDPP), has a monitoring role. He has administered the program for 4 years before turning his attention to perceived inequities in the disbursement of training grants. Although WDPP was set up to satisfy specific constituencies, namely, public, not-for-profit, and private organizations, there are data to support the fact that private businesses were the chief beneficiaries. The perception of inequity is compounded by the fact that the training grant decisions are not made in an open, transparent manner. Jim Corliss now faces the prospect of having to provide oral and written reports to the elected officials regarding the agency's activities over the past 4 years as well as offer plans for the future.

The report should provide information concerning the demands made on the agency (primarily from private businesses); the number and type of training awards made over time; management of the training awards program with an emphasis on the challenges—in particular, those related to the uncertainty of the extent of the financial resources and the implications of this uncertainty for planning and implementing the program; and proposed changes to the policy, structures, and strategies to facilitate more efficient and effective use of funds made available to the agency.

The way Jim presents the data is important. He should highlight the fact that over the past 4 years the number of applications received from small, minority- and female-owned firms has decreased, while the number of applications from large private-sector firms seeking ISO funding has increased exponentially and as a result these large organizations are the primary beneficiaries of WDPP funds. Let the data speak for themselves. The elected officials can't fault the companies who figured out the government would help pay for ISO training. Rather, they can place a cap on the number of ISO training grants awarded, which appears to be an obvious alternative, although politically unwise. The elected officials, ever cognizant of their reelection efforts, need to keep campaign contributions in mind.

So in addition to the cap on ISO awards, WDPP needs to figure out a way to increase the number of applications from smaller companies. They need to communicate more effectively with the small, minority- and female-owned companies to inform them about the availability of training dollars for displaced workers. WDPP should provide technical assistance to the smaller companies, who are typically understaffed, to help them develop competitive proposals and quality training programs. Jim should attempt to learn why the smaller companies are not applying for the funds by talking with representatives of small and medium-sized firms around the state. He could make individual phone calls or he could hold round-table discussions as a way not only to learn why the small and medium-sized companies aren't applying for training grants, but to also generate new ideas. Do these companies lack the capacity, or does the financial match turn them away? If capacity is the response, then technical assistance may very well be the answer. If the required match is the answer, then the dollar for dollar match should be revisited. A formula for matching funds could be developed where the larger, wealthier firms provide a 100% match, while the smaller companies provide a 50% or 25% match.

The proposed changes are likely to generate more interest and applications for WDPP funds and enable the organization to distribute the funds more equitably. It's possible that the effort to increase communication with the companies that do business in the state will facilitate greater openness and transparency in the agencies' activities. In a move to have a more open and transparent system for making training award decisions, the WDPP should consider the establishment of a review committee composed of a diverse cross section of business leaders to review the applications with WDPP staff and make recommendations for funding. In addition, WDPP should publicize the names of the companies receiving funding and the purpose of their training efforts, as well as the number of displaced workers benefiting from the training.

Hedy Isaacs is a lecturer at the University of the West Indies, Mona Campus, in Kingston, Jamaica.

Willy McCourt

The first thing Jim should do is understand what his program is for, in economic and political terms. Economically, the program is a response to the movement of U.S. manufacturing jobs overseas, especially to Asia. Arguably, the correct response is for the United States to give up on volume manufacturing and move up-market into high-value service and research-led economic activity.

Politically, Jim's program is a way for the government to show that it has a response to the decline in manufacturing jobs. That response may well be gestural: Politicians may merely want to show that they are doing something, however ineffectual.

Be that as it may, Jim is working at the level where most of us are, handed a program and obliged to make the best of a bad job. What to do at this level?

I would encourage Jim to scale down the ISO program. Is there evidence that ISO (as opposed to an internally led, noncertificated total quality management program) improves quality, other than in areas where a standard for all organizations to reach can be specified unambiguously? I've not seen it. Thus, Jim should reverse the drift of spending toward ISO.

It makes perfect sense for an individual company, obliged to compete, to get the ISO certification. It makes no sense for a government agency to encourage companies in general to go for it, to the extent that ISO merely represents a badge of status.

What is the most effective way for an agency like Jim's to assist unemployed workers and to help employers to create jobs? Where the workers are concerned, I would encourage Jim to put as much money in their hands as possible. Running schemes for the unemployed costs money in itself (what economists call a transaction cost): People like Jim have to be paid, and that is at the expense of the unemployed themselves. The money, however, should arguably not be in the form of weekly unemployment relief (I assume that something of the sort already exists), which will be used for current consumption, but in the form of a lump sum, which might be earmarked for training or business start-up activity.

As for help to the companies, I think the large companies can look after themselves. For the small and medium-sized enterprises (SMEs), Jim should ask them what kind of help they would most appreciate. Subject to what they reply, I would look at the breaks that can be given to SMEs to take on unemployed workers. Government regulations and tax systems may make it hard for them to do so.

I would also develop the advice Jim's agency gives to SMEs in how to train their workers. This is something that SMEs often neglect, and government can facilitate it.

Finally, the institutional framework for Jim's agency needs to be reformed to get politicians' hands off operational decisions. I am a democrat, but I also believe in the doctrine of separation between elected and appointed officials. The politicians should determine the strategic orientation of the program and then get out of the way. It follows that Jim should use his influence so that his successor is a professional and not a political appointee. His own appointment is an example of the politicization of public appointments down to a quite low level that is a negative feature of American public administration. As in this case, it results in the use of public funds to buy off special interest groups.

Real people are suffering from the loss of their factory jobs, so any help that Jim can offer to the unemployed will be very worth while. He should deliver these proposals at the upcoming meeting.

Willy McCourt is a professor at the University of Manchester in England.

Ethel Williams

The situation faced by Jim Corliss in preparing for his upcoming meeting is certainly a difficult one. The current trend of decreasing applications from not-for-profit organizations coupled with the low number of grant recipients from small and minority businesses paints a less than perfect picture of the grant decisions made under the Workforce Development Partnership Program (WDPP). Nevertheless, in preparing for the meeting with elected officials Jim must be as honest in his presentation as possible. Jim should use the current program and economic difficulties as an opportunity for programmatic changes. The key to making the meeting successful is to use the elected officials as a catalyst for the much needed changes. Jim Corliss should consider the following points in preparing and presenting past activities and future plans.

Past Activities

Past funding decisions were based primarily on one part of the WDPP's twofold function. Most grants were made to "eligible employing organizations for their own training purposes." The emphasis on customized training and subsequent ISO certification can be presented as both an advantage and a disadvantage. Positively speaking, individuals in the community have received necessary retraining, while local companies have produced the quality products associated with ISO certification. The status associated with ISO certification can also be used to attract businesses to the area for economic development purposes. The elected officials should be reminded, however, that their support for many business and industry leaders and subsequent grant recommendations for those businesses has contributed to the current imbalance in grantee organizations. The need for "fairness and ethical concerns as well as fiscal responsibility" is a responsibility of both WDPP and elected representatives in the community. Corliss should present this as an opportunity for those present to discuss, and perhaps suggest ways of developing, alternatives that would emphasize the second function of WDPP: payment for retraining eligible displaced workers. This may be a way to increase the number of small business, minority business, and not-for-profit applications.

Future Plans

Future plans should carefully consider the matching requirements for grant recipients. Perhaps the elected officials may be helpful in exploring feasible alternatives. Alternatives for balancing payment to organizations for the actual retraining of workers versus payment for customized training (especially ISO certification) must be considered. The manner in which eligibility requirements are determined in this area should be carefully reviewed. Additional points can be given for retraining versus certification. Also, additional consideration should be given to organizations that can show they will not relocate within 5 years. The questions raised by Jim concerning competitive bidding among ISO experts determining the credentials of ISO experts may be too political and too tenuous to address at this meeting. Perhaps working from the positive question of increasing individual retraining and balancing the two-pronged responsibility of WDPP may be a better approach.

To better enhance WDPP's ability to manage funds, allocation deadlines can be changed. Final grant decisions should be made after actual government revenues are received. The manner in which Corliss presents this information can be a determinant in judging past activities and projecting future success.

Ethel Williams teaches public administration at the University of Nebraska at Omaha.

Case 15 Comments: Getting the Staff On Board

What Is Wrong and What Should Be Done?

Tae Hoe Eom

The City of Moyenne is facing many socioeconomic issues, and Nicholas Guerin, the new city manager, is at the stage of initiating creative ways to handle those issues. Since Nicholas lacks very detailed information on the issues in the city, and analyzing advantages and disadvantages of proposals is the first step to choosing which development project to implement, he definitely needs to collect diverse opinions from the Community Development Department director and her department managers. But he did not receive various opinions; instead, the department director's voice was echoed by the managers. As usual, many underlying organizational factors could have caused such problems; formal and informal organizational structure, authority, leadership, and communication should be areas we should focus on for analysis. However, the most obvious fact, at least on the surface, is that the Community Development Department is suffering from an excessively rigid organizational atmosphere and inflexible communication.

One way of viewing an organization is to consider it as an elaborate system for gathering, evaluating, synthesizing, and disseminating information. The communication structure of an organization is a network of human relationships, a linkage of subordinates to superiors, running from every person at the bottom of the structure to the person at the top. As such, communication plays a very basic but extremely crucial role for organizational effectiveness. It is involved in every stage of the new development projects the City of Moyenne is planning: initiating, evaluating, selecting, and implementing proposals. More important is creating a voluntary consensus among managers by getting through those processes.

Nicholas Guerin should find out the sources of such communication problems. Potential barriers to effective communication in this situation include:

1. *Authority/Power:* Does the formal organizational structure provide too much authority or power to Jane Hernandez, director of the Community Development Department, or does her personality dominate the departments' atmosphere? First, Nicholas needs to know whether it is due to personal leadership or structural problems. If it is due to the formal organizational structure, he needs to look into the flow of the power and communication routes between and in the departments.

2. *Group Loyalties:* An organization also has different subcultures. Nicholas needs to analyze what unique subculture the Community Development Department has.

3. *Motivation:* If the managers anticipate that their proposals would not be successfully implemented because of, for example, budget problems or political leverage, they are most likely to lose their motivation to analyze and activate the proposals. Lack of incentives or individual and/or department political responsibility for the proposals might be reasons for the "safe and lukewarm" attitude in the department.

Analyzing those factors may take a long time for Nicholas, who has a short deadline for reporting to the council. The first thing Nicholas should do, then, is to clearly state what his performance expectations are to Jane and her managers. An informal brainstorming session might help Nicholas get what he wants. One caveat is that the idea already presented by Jane should not be dismissed simply because it is not brand new. Nicholas should find out why they repeated the proposal; it might be a result of intensive brainstorming previously done by the department.

Tae Ho Eom is a doctoral candidate at Syracuse University.

Ray Gonzales

The problem seems to be something akin to a "bad vibe" in the organization. That is, the general mood of the department, if not the organization, does not seem to be conducive to high productivity. On the face of it, Jane seems to be an important part of the problem. Closely looking at the issue, however, may hint at something a little deeper. Social interaction is often governed by personality/psychology, communication traits and skills, timing, and context. Jane's ostensible dominance could be the result of any combination of these things. Is Jane a control freak or is she the lone enthusiast surrounded by sheep? Nick's perspective, while informed by intuition and experience, is undoubtedly incomplete. Nevertheless, let's trust it for the sake of this writing.

Talent and ego. The worst combination is to have too little of the former and a whole bunch of the latter. People with big egos are terrible coworkers—holding on, life and limb, to their titles and insisting on being respected because of them. Insofar as public organizations are concerned, they miss the point of their own existence in an effort to preserve an outward appearance. The costs can be, and often are, considerable.

One symptom is an inability to distinguish between an argument and verbal aggression. An argumentative exchange is one in which ideas are attacked. In verbally aggressive encounters, a person's self-concept is ridiculed. No-talent, fat-egoed people regard any attack on an idea of theirs as a personal attack. In the present study, if the managers in the room are familiar with Jane's tendency to get defensive when her ideas are threatened, the type of desirable work environment described by Nick will be prohibited. Further, everyone is likely to sit around saying nothing.

As of a few years ago, people weak in argumentative skills generally experience more communication maladies such as problems maintaining relationships and higher incidents of verbal aggression than persons relatively high in argumentation skills. People see highly argumentative people as being more intelligent, and they usually have high self-esteem. Nick's coworkers at his former place of employment most likely were highly argumentative, highly engaged, and probably didn't feel like committing hari kari if someone bashed one of their ideas.

On the other hand, I think it is also important to try to understand Jane in relation to her managers and coworkers. Is she noticeably younger than the people she supervises? Is she the only woman? What is her management style like? Who was her mentor? Things like this can affect the character of a leader and Nick's interpretation of the meeting.

What should Nick do?

This sounds like a cop-out, but, as in romance, he needs to play to his strengths. The solution is different for everyone. He needs to go with whatever made him successful to begin with—personality, intelligence, aggressiveness, looks, luck. Senior managers should have a pretty good sense of themselves and should work to emphasize the good stuff to get what they need. That said, I have a few more practical recommendations.

Create an environment conducive to argument. This involves being more of a teacher than a manager. Get people to understand that argument is not a bad thing. To the extent possible, I like the idea of formal training in debate. It doesn't necessarily have to be verbal either. A leader should cultivate the mental skill set associated with debating, not necessarily the verbal ability itself. Make sure they know that there's nothing wrong with being wrong.

Lead by example and be grounded. This doesn't mean that people need to walk around pretending everything is wonderful, but there is a certain sense of community and a feeling that we are all in this together when the most formally influential people prefer to be called by their first name. There is no intimidation. No "I'm better than you." Leadership needs to articulate a vision for the organization and then work to get everyone to buy into that vision. Make it known that there is no success without everyone's input. Then practice what you preach.

While somewhat narrow, these are just a couple of things that can be done to help. If Nick is focused, and makes the best use of his own natural ability, his staff can realize true organizational unity and increasing levels of productivity. And if that doesn't work . . . fire Jane.

Ray Gonzales, PhD, works in administration at USC in Los Angeles and teaches public administration on the side.

Ton van der Wiel

Nicholas faces a classic problem: The (political) ambitions voiced in the organization do not automatically match the standard working and procedures (the culture). There's a huge gap between what they want and what they actually do. More specific, there is a gap between the political and bureaucratic/professional ambitions in Moyenne.

Nicholas perhaps made a few mistakes as well. He seems not to have been alert to the possibility of this gap while he was getting the job. Now he's caught by surprise. Furthermore, he made the mistake of assuming that Moyenne is like Monplaisir. In the way he solicited input through Jane, he intended to trigger some wild brainstorming as he was used to in Monplaisir. What a good memory he has of that! Instead, he reinforced the standard hierarchy in Moyenne. What a bad score . . .

So he has two problems:

1. He has to come up with some creative and diverse ideas within a month, working with people who use a different interpretation of their professionalism.

2. He will have to transform the culture of the organization.

What to Do?

Facing his deadline, he needs short-term action. He needs to organize and facilitate a process in which he changes the context and focus of the standard operations of Mrs. Hernandez and her soldiers. He hires a bus and goes on tour. For two days he and the Hernandez brigade go out and have an excursion to the hotspots of interest. It is only them, a personal assistant to Nicholas, some little scraps of paper, and a flip chart. They stop at the polluted areas and dangerous and rundown neighborhoods and they deliberately drive into a traffic jam, and so on. At each and every stop they put up a little camp for deliberation. Nicholas runs them through a simple set of questions. Our professionals first write down their short answers to the questions; after that they read out their answers in turn, and the results are collected on a flip chart.

The questions are, in the given situation (i.e., traffic jam):

- What is the issue we're facing?
- What is the challenge?

- Starting from your issue and challenge, give three options or opportunities to explore.
- Give three actions we can take tomorrow.

Camping in the bus or on the pavement (we hope the weather is good), the context of work-related questions is shifted and the focus is very specific. The input is collected and only briefly discussed before they go to the next bus stop. Finally they arrive at that fine grand café of Moyenne: "l'Autre Monde." Over a drink or two (or three) they discuss some of the things that happened. Nicholas comes up with some more scraps of paper and asks everyone to give only one or two insights or ideas their tour of the city brought to them.

He thanks them for this journey and they leave. A day later he and his assistant report back to the Hernandez group the results of the day. Now Nicholas has something to work with to meet his deadline.

Changing the culture of Moyenne has started. Surely Nicholas will not have solved this problem by going on tour. He will have to come up with more initiatives in which his own behavior must be an example. Something of a plan still has to be made. He did, however, offer the Hernandez brigade an experience they liked. People are asking him when they can have a tour. Transforming the bureaucracy of Moyenne from an inward-looking hierarchy into an outward-oriented professional organization has started.

Ton van der Wiel is the manager of the Dutch Bureau for Innovative Policy Making (XPIN).

Case 16 Comments: Starting the New Job

What Is Wrong and What Should Be Done?

Domonic A. Bearfield

Despite Linda's great opportunity, I believe that this may not be the best time for her to accept the position. Perhaps the largest issue is the health of her spouse. Because of the uncertainty surrounding his condition, and the concern regarding the transfer of health benefits, it appears that the outside distractions are already starting to impact her performance. If this is truly the opportunity that she has been waiting most of her professional career for, then she should approach it with a mind free of distractions. Because of the increased profile, a poor performance can have ramifications that could impact the rest of her career. At the very least, I would suggest she delay her employment until she has a better handle on her husband's medical condition.

Should she decide to stay, however, there are several significant challenges that she will have to deal with immediately. I am dismayed by the changes occurring in the organization. It appears that the line of communication among employees needs to be improved. In many ways, the description of the building, isolated and set apart, serves as a metaphor for the employees within. The organization has to do a better job of showing employees the value of working together and improving communication. Just like the windowless views from within the office, it appears that the employees are so focused on their individual tasks that they are missing how they are connected to the outside world. Also, as demonstrated by the "my typewriter" incident, and the comment suggesting that Linda will have to "know who's been doing what . . . ," a great deal of energy will have to be expended to make sure that the level of trust among employees is addressed and repaired. Because of the "brain drain" caused by retiring employees, this is a time of tremendous upheaval and uncertainty. It may take some time to find out where the gaps in knowledge and experience are within the organization. But it is also an opportunity to reinvent the culture. Both of these tasks will be daunting.

I know this job has a tremendous upside for Linda professionally. In many ways it appears that she has been working her whole career for this opportunity. However, I do not think that this is the best fit for her at this time. Because of the uncertain situation with her family, the changes at the new organization, and the unstable nature of the position (it is a political, at-will appointment), I suggest that she decline the job offer at this time.

Domonic A. Bearfield teaches public administration at the University of New Hampshire.

Jon Foster Pedley

Before anything else, Linda should take a (metaphorical) long walk and think hard about what she wants. She has an ill husband, security offered to her by her old job, and great peer and boss relations there. But she also has the possibility of great professional growth in her new job, albeit with significant personal, professional, and emotional challenges. She isn't going anywhere until she's sure of what she wants and has come to a fundamental understanding of what home/life balance she needs, especially in this time of medical crisis with her husband.

She should ask herself, looking back in 10 years, of what choice does she think she will she be most proud?

If she chooses family and spouse support as her primary goal now, then her old job is alluring: good medical aid, peer and boss support, challenge, and enough security to allow more attention to family health challenges. She's talented, has integrity, and may have later opportunities—or even make them for herself. She'll grow through this too.

If, on the other hand, she chooses the new professional growth challenge, then she needs to establish her presence and imprint her modus operandi and beliefs on her new organization without delay. For her own psychic ease and to free her energies, she would be wise to ensure that she and her partner agree about this way forward and understand the potential risks and costs. And why not take the opportunity to test this new organization at an early stage—can it deliver or not?

Phase one is to establish her presence. Ted, the HR director, needs to know what's at stake here and to understand that for the good of the organization as a whole he has to deliver fast action in transferring Linda's health benefits. For what is at stake should be Linda's continuation with this job. Already the new director has waited several months for Linda—they clearly need her, and if their impatience to recruit her is not matched by an ability to deliver on crucial issues, then it's important they know they will lose her. That simple. Some issues are nonnegotiable and this is one. While Linda risks some alienation here she also will make it clear that she is a player whose positions are serious and must be respected. Linda, tactfully, must clarify a timeline on this and stick to it.

She has two other points on which she needs to establish a presence. The first is with her new boss. Obviously, delivering on her boss's request for the funding reallocations would create a good working confidence between them. But it's not that clear-cut. She's inducting Linda badly.

Linda needs more from her boss than she's getting in order to get up and running. It's in Linda's hands: She needs to schedule a time to meet with her boss in the next day or two to clarify expectations and to ask questions that she needs answers to. Linda's boss, like all managers, gets results through people, and she'd better start exhibiting some management skills to get results through Linda. Maybe she is preoccupied, unaware—who knows—maybe she has some family health problems too. Linda had better take the initiative here and engage in a conversation that not only clarifies her issues but also poses a few questions that allow her boss to think a little—it doesn't sound like she has much chance of that, and she may welcome it.

The second place to establish a presence is with her team.

Linda has to be authentic here. She's a good leader, it appears, and may be able to create vision and direction. But now she needs to practice these talents at Olympic level. She must show confidence in her team and bring them together.

She has two gifts presented to her to help. The first is the general uncertainty in the organization. She can clarify the challenges, show the necessity for new ways of acting, inevitable due to the change of administration, and in some ways escalate the uncertainties to a sense of crisis—to which she can encourage her team to respond.

Second, she's aided by the opportunity provided by the project her boss has handed her. If her team pulls together and handles this well, then budgets will be increased and there may be more funds for training, visits to other departments, resources, and staff. Together they can achieve a real success for themselves. So Linda needs to get her team to understand this, stay hands-off but enabling, and demonstrate trust in their abilities to deliver the analysis, and so on. Then she needs to show her capability to apply theory to the data they've produced and make powerful arguments to support improvements—and if successful she is being delivered the possibility of a quick win, on a plate.

With all this, she will win her team's support, her boss's confidence, and more resources—and then can start working on her longer-term projects: reconstruction, new offices, better facilities, etc.

If this is what she wants . . .

Jon Foster Pedley is a senior lecturer in the Graduate School of Business at the University of Cape Town.

Navdeep Mathur

This case gives an account of difficulties faced by a very skilled and experienced public manager. Linda has 20 years' experience in her field and has established a reputation for successfully facing challenges and establishing positive relationships while at it. As a consequence, she has been appointed to a key position in a department in her professional field. She has been particularly chosen for her people skills (i.e., interpersonal communication, problem solving, and negotiation skills). However, she feels worried, uncertain, and overwhelmed about her new assignment. The chief problem here is her husband's ill health and the ramifications in terms of large medical treatment costs. The family concerns are the main reason she feels distracted and unable to feel fully confident of her potential.

There are a number of things she needs to do to manage her worries about her family and put her best foot forward in the new assignment. The first priority is to have a clear discussion with Ted, the HR director, about the medical plan. If this discussion includes her own director, it could be a more beneficial discussion so that everyone understands that in order for her to do her job well, she needs the pressure of medical costs to be alleviated. Given that the new medical plan is good— a solid reassurance that even if papers move slowly, her husband's medical treatment will be covered to her satisfaction—this is an important move to get Linda to focus on the new assignment at hand.

Linda's staff seems to be less than organized as far as a mission is concerned. There seems to be some mutual distrust and general boredom with their work areas. She would benefit by putting her people skills to work over the next few days, having several one-on-one meetings with staff members. By allowing each member to share information in confidence with her, they will have the opportunity to "have a rant" and then get on with it. Linda might consider transferring any staff member who she thinks will not be a willing participant in the new assignment, such as the member who requested to have a more "regional role." They may be more productive in an area of their choice.

With staff issues a bit clearer, she should make an attempt to develop them as a team—this might mean a social event away from the office but not necessarily a standard "team building away-day." Such a social event may be followed up with regular informal meetings of small groups of staff where she lays out the tasks that need to be done for each part of the new project. This series of meetings would also be a good opportunity to develop informal yet well-ordered medium-term and daily procedures. Since there is no room big enough for the entire staff or even a floor of staff, Linda should split them into subgroups, based on the area of the office where they sit, and then gradually remake such groups on the basis on their expertise and location in the new project.

At the same time, she should engage in discussion with her director and others who share her views about the changes required in the department's work and policy issues in the broader professional area. This sharing of a common commitment and reinforcing the main purpose of the department under this new administration may bring back some of the enthusiasm to get on with a new ambitious work program that is otherwise characterized as "dispirited." This way, her tense boss may find it easier to open up and develop a better working relationship with Linda, hopefully resulting in a well-thought-out discussion about the priorities for which budgetary allocations are planned.

Having fleshed out staff issues, and with a greater sense of security about the mission of others in the department, Linda now needs her staff to work out important bits of research from their files. While institutional memory cannot be jogged without the members who held it, it is possible for fairly skilled professionals to pull their informational resources and prepare relevant reports, with Linda applying her theory-application skills to position them toward the urgent project. In a relatively short span of time, she will begin to make greater progress toward this end.

With these major moves underway, Linda finds out that there are several large conference rooms available a short drive away for agency departments to hold meetings. She then schedules one 3-hour meeting a week at such a venue to note progress on the work program as well as get feedback from staff. She chooses to deal with individual problems separately, calling a staff member to her office during the week, but uses this meeting to address in depth different stages of the project and its progress and identify the major tasks remaining. This would also be a good opportunity to appreciate her staff for coming together on this major project soon after she joined. After this meeting, the entire staff along with Linda would have lunch in the staff cafeteria in the same building. This gives them an opportunity to get to know staff members in other related departments and gradually build working relationships with them.

With Linda taking these small steps toward success in the new assignment, the worst case scenario is that the work may not get done on time, and this big opportunity may be missed. Given the dismal environment that existed prior to Linda's arrival, it would be hard for anyone to actually place the blame squarely on her shoulders, yet the strides taken toward the project's goals would hardly go unnoticed. By this time, she not only would be more settled in the job but also would have created a research and staff base for the longer term, in addition to forthcoming projects. And the medical plan would have begun paying the bills.

Navdeep Mathur is a research fellow with the Institute for Local Government Studies School of Public Policy at the University of Birmingham, UK.

Case 17 Comments:
Friendships and the Job

What Is Wrong and What Should Be Done?

Seok-Hwan Lee

You lost your best colleague, but you remain in your workplace. What does this mean?

This case provides us with important motivational issues among employees in an era of limited resources. Whether it is called downsizing, layoffs, or cutback management, it is the strategic act of reducing the size of an organization's workforce. Its ultimate goal is to do more with less—realizing efficiencies by pruning both labor and capital.

Probably, the easiest way to improve productivity and efficiency is to mechanize the processes and structures, while cutting people. It may be a good way to enhance efficiency in the short term. However, the most difficult and endurable way to increase the level of productivity is to get a high level of commitment from employees. Even if we have best processes and structures, it is almost impossible to achieve the intended goal unless people are cooperative and supportive.

From such a point of view, the main problem here is employees' low morale. Taking everything into account, the following problems can appear in the company. Although the intended goal of layoffs is to enhance productivity, the unexpected costs listed below may stifle employees' motivational bases, thereby eventually decreasing productivity.

1. *Grief and Anger:* Ming, who went through his shock, experiences high degrees of grief and anger.

2. *Fear and Distrust:* Loss of trust in management is the most predictable problem. Ming observes that good employees are among the casualties.

Office politics is more important than real performance to determine who stays on. He no longer trusts the CEO.

3. *Workplace Hostility:* Ming no longer thinks his workplace is friendly.

4. *Excessive Stress:* Stress is a psychological response to perceived threat. Ming began to realize some possible problems in this case. He will eventually suffer from job overload, role ambiguity, and concerns about family and work balance.

5. *Higher Turnover:* Employees are resigning. Survivors of corporate restructurings are voluntarily leaving their organizations. So can we really say we will be productive?

What the CEO Ought to Do

Since the layoff has unintended costs, it can be detrimental to employee moral, thereby decreasing productivity in the long term. Meanwhile, it is inevitable for the company to go through this financial difficulty since the situation is given as an environmental factor. If necessary, the layoffs must be done in a detailed and organized way.

First, it is important to have sufficient time to inform employees of what is happening. In a downsizing environment, tension between top management and employees is likely to occur. Since the layoffs are likely to produce the problems mentioned above, it is critical for top management to give people the necessary time to be aware of what is happening in their organization and why.

Second, the CEO must establish exemption criteria before staff reduction. A well-organized downsizing plan should begin with the objective identification of excess employees. While ambiguous performance increases conflicts and tensions among employees, and it is difficult to secure clear performance measures, establishing exemption criteria reduces the pool of potentially excess employees and helps identify what is important for the organization.

Third, the CEO must make sure that the company has transparent communication systems. During any period of staff reduction, the maintenance of honest, open, and frequent communication by an effective leader can contribute to a more effective and humane outcome. Many success stories show that openness and honesty about the reason for, and the process of, staff reduction were critical in the layoffs.

Finally, the company should place the emphasis on reinvestment and redeployment.

After the transparent communication, sufficient time, and detailed exemption criteria, excess staff detection is directly linked to redeployment first, not to retrenchment.

What Ming Should Do

Although Ming feels bad in this situation, he can tell the CEO about the contribution that Gurav made for the company and ask if there is any way for him to be redeployed. If this is not acceptable, Ming should start to look for another job, as there is no way for his work motivation to be restored. He may remain in the company. But this is not good for him because there is no hope for this company to be a pleasant workplace. Trust is gone, and there is no reason to stay unless he fails to find a new job.

Seok-Hwan Lee teaches public administration at the Catholic University of Korea, South Korea.

Carl W. Nelson

Perspective on the Work Organization

Caliber Technologies, a small software development company, is a contractor of the National Economic Development Agency (NEDA). The company had missed its fourth-quarter targets and NEDA was pressing for a definite product delivery date. An emergency board of directors meeting had been held the previous evening to deal with a looming cash flow problem.

The focal areas of Caliber's software development efforts and the number of current or potential customers beyond its contract with NEDA are not clear. As a small organization that appears to be dependent on the creative skills and talents of its software engineers, there is no evidence that Caliber's management is acting systematically or strategically: Three indicators of a lack of a systematic and strategic approach by Caliber's leadership are

- Ming, Gurav, and the other employees' lack of awareness of the critical situation should Caliber miss its fourth-quarter numbers;
- no evidence of strategic plans or efforts to expand its customer base to cushion itself if the company cannot meet or satisfy NEDA's expectations; and
- the absence of explicit performance review processes.

Reactive Actions of the Board of Directors

Faced with a near-term cash flow crisis, the board's actions are a reasonable response to an unplanned crisis from their perspective. Reduce costs and make sure the current product in development gets out the door. Development was near completion so it made sense to cut more staff from the development part of the organization than from the sales and marketing side. Including Gurav in the staff reduction could be justified on the following grounds:

- The project was nearly done so Gurav's creativity and experience were less critical.
- As one of the first hires, his salary was probably higher than salaries of more recent hires.
- Gurav's poor working relationship with his new manager undercut management's perception of him as a team player.

Ming's Connections With Gurav

It will be hard for Ming to evaluate the overall situation objectively because of the following:

- Ming and Gurav had been friends since their college years.
- Gurav helped Ming get his first job.
- They had roomed together for years.
- They commuted to work together in Gurav's car.
- Ming perceived Gurav as one of Caliber's more creative and effective developers.
- The five-member team in which they worked had developed a camaraderie.
- Gurav had mentored Ming at Caliber and helped him when he was frustrated with his programming efforts.

A Perspective That Ming Is Not Likely to Have

While employees generally perceive organizations from a personalized point of view, the majority of organizational actions are generally best understood from a systems perspective. From this broader perspective, the reduction in force was a systems response, not one based on office politics or personalities. Gurav's poor relationship with his new manager may have influenced the decision to let him go, but it probably was not the determining factor. Cost savings and near-term product completion were the likely driving forces.

What Should Ming Do?

Ming should stay put and keep up his efforts for many reasons:

- Quitting his job to protest Gurav's termination would not serve any useful purpose because management would not view it as a protest of letting good people go. If Ming were to quit, his action would be viewed as a lack of understanding of Caliber's situation.

- Putting in less effort to protest would also be perceived negatively because getting the product finished and out the door is Caliber's most urgent need. Management would react negatively if Ming were perceived as hindering product completion.

• No one has stated explicitly that the layoffs were permanent. If Caliber survives the near-term crisis, they may be willing to consider rehiring Gurav because of his creativity and experience. By staying with the organization and pulling his share of the load, Ming will be in a good position to determine if there should be any opportunity for Gurav to return.

• Gurav has been with the company long enough to have unemployment benefits, and Ming needs to continue working to help cover their housing costs until Gurav finds new employment.

• Ming acted wisely in e-mailing his friends and family to instruct them to send personal e-mails to his nonwork account. When under stress, an organization looks more negatively on frequent personal e-mails than they do in less stressful situations.

It's a good thing Ming does not have a ride immediately available because he should not leave work because a good friend was let go. It is even possible that Gurav will return to give him a ride home. As Ming and Gurav had not been able to talk before the all-staff meeting, Gurav may have additional information that will help Ming better understand the situation. And while Ming understandably views Gurav's termination as a "bad" event, recent research has shown how quickly most individuals (both Ming and Gurav) adapt to both good and bad experiences and move on with their lives.

Carl W. Nelson, PhD, is the manager of planning, monitoring and evaluation for the Department of Services for Children, Youth and Their Families, State of Delaware.

Francine Widrich

If Ming is considering quitting his job or, worse yet, sabotaging his employer because his friend was laid off, he is letting his friendship with Gurav cloud his judgment. Ming should be appreciative to Gurav for helping him get a job with this company, but he needs to remember that his talents and skills were the reasons he was hired.

Ming should consider that the company did not meet its earnings expectations and that this will lead to future financial difficulties for the company. The decision to dismiss Gurav was not based on his poor performance; it was based on the company's poor performance. Employees nonessential to the company were the target of the layoff. If the company fails to act when faced with financial difficulties, all employees are at risk of losing their jobs.

If, however, the company's looming financial difficulties were bogus and Gurav was laid off because of his performance, Ming still does not have a cause for action. He knew that Gurav's relationship with his manager, Ivan, was not very good. It was "marked by passive-aggressive behaviors, backstabbing, and resentment." Since Ming and Gurav worked for different managers, Ming did not know if Gurav was the cause of the problems. Ming most likely only heard Gurav's side of the story. While we all would like to think that our friends are easy to get along with and are great at everything they do, this assumption is not always right. Gurav might have been a great friend to Ming, but he might not have been great for the company.

At this point, however, Ming should be happy he was not the one who lost his job. And it is good that Ming decided to redirect his e-mails; he was using his work e-mail account to receive personal e-mails, including questionable forwards and inappropriate jokes. The board of directors might not think Ming is essential to the organization if they knew he had time for this kind of stuff.

Francine Widrich is an administrator at the New Jersey Division of Consumer Affairs.

Case 18 Comments:
The Workplace of Doom

What Is Wrong and What Should Be Done?

Raphael J. Caprio

Dominic. Dominic. Dominic. While it is hard to believe that in this day and age it would be difficult to consider the likelihood of "workplaces of doom" existing, they do, and often in surprising numbers. The number of sexual, violent, and generic harassing workplace litigations is again increasing after a brief, 3-year period during which the number of new cases seemed to have leveled off. Regrettably, they are on the increase again and increasing at rates faster than in the past.

There are a couple of different perspectives one can take on this harassing workplace experience. Let's start with the realities.

Most often, failure to prevent workplace aggression, manifested in its many guises, is not due to inadequate policies and risk management practices. Virtually every major institution, business, or employer has policies and processes in place to deal with the type of narcissistic aggrandizement and manipulation practiced by "MC." Why, then, if policies exist, with practices in place, do these "compliance programs" fail?

The problem generally lies in "human error." When hidden risk factors are ignored, employees fail to use the protections that are in place, to their personal detriment and to the detriment of the institution or company. In this particular case, there were signals, patterns, and keys, obvious from virtually the day Dominic set foot in his dream job: "Lisa, would you bring us some coffee, dear?" ". . . *that* neighborhood." There are no employees to MC, only trophies and subservient peons: "I can't wait to show you off."

Until recently, what was not known was that there are a host of hidden risk factors for workplace aggression and harassment. Lacking this information, there has also been a concurrent lack of commonly known strategies to reduce exposure to litigation and financial loss and to secondary exposures such as negative work climate, employee attrition, and reduced worker productivity. We now know that the following are several of the many risk factors for harassment in the workplace:

- Victims fail to use employer's procedural protections more often than they use them, despite training and education.
- Women perceive a different set of behaviors as harassing compared to men.
- Harassers, such as MC, almost never perceive their behavior as harassing.
- The majority of workers perceive retaliation as a likely consequence of coming forward, regardless of prohibitions against it.
- Supervisors almost uniformly believe that they will not be supported by their superiors if they side with a plaintiff.

In this particular instance, matters were likely exacerbated because it is entirely likely that MC's position, continued survival, and arrogance reflected a much wider systemic problem within the organization. He would not have been able to continue without tacit support from above. Accordingly, the only assumption I will make is that this institution effectively "allowed" this behavior to continue even though it is also reasonable to assume that the agency had compliance programs and policies designed to prevent the behavior exhibited by MC.

So where does that leave Dominic? Not with many easy or pretty choices.

Dominic needs to recognize that he is finished at this agency. He has no future there for a couple of reasons. First, he has already been marginalized by MC. Second, he needs to recognize he is in this place in part because of his own inability to recognize predatory behavior and his inability to deal with it in an effective manner. It's difficult to point out that many individuals become victims because of their own inexperience or naiveté, which may land them in harm's way, without it appearing to be a case of blaming the victim, which I'm not trying to do. I'm only trying to indicate that employees at all levels have a responsibility to assert their rights and must do so before situations devolve into hopelessness. In addition, however regrettable, there are times when even with the best efforts to prevent being abused, situations do deteriorate.

Third, if Dominic chooses to take some sort of action, given the implicit support MC must have, he will inevitably be labeled as a trouble-maker, going nowhere fast. Fourth, if he does not succeed in displacing MC or securing some sort of compensation, he will not likely receive any sort of recommendation or cooperation with interagency transfers. Fifth, if he succeeds, he will still be perceived as the trouble-maker who upset the old boy network, again with no future—employed perhaps, but with no future at the agency.

What to do? Aggressively seek other employment while you can still do so on your own terms. Build the case against MC as you do so: the paper trail, the harassing behavior, the duplicity, the arbitrary and capricious behavior. Finally, do the right thing. Bring down MC, but on your way out, on your own terms.

Raphael J. Caprio is the vice president for continuous education and outreach and professor of public administration at Rutgers University.

Annie Hondeghem

The main problem in this case is the behavior of the boss, MC. He has a very paternalistic attitude, manipulates his personnel in order to keep control, and humiliates them. Examples of this are:
Paternalistic attitude:

- Making comments on the neighborhood where Dominic is living
- Arranging membership in clubs
- Taking over the chair of meetings
- Not listening to Dominic's arguments

Manipulating:

- Influencing decisions of meetings until they suit him
- Isolating Dominic from his colleagues and setting people up against each other by telling them they are incompetent
- Beating and caressing at the same time
- Considering Dominic a good worker as long as Dominic is useful to him (first year) but casting him away when he is considered no longer useful

Humiliation:

- Shouting at the secretary to bring coffee
- Introducing Dominic as being "only an employee"
- Spying
- Telling Dominic that he is a square peg in a round hole, without any real argument

Although the behavior of the boss is the most important problem, I think there is also a problem with Dominic himself. He has walked into a trap because of personal commitments. As he bought a very expensive house (in accordance with his standing as an executive) and as his wife has given up her job, he has reduced the number of alternatives to organize his life. He can no longer say, "I will look for another job" because he has become too dependent upon this one and his high salary. It takes a lot of time, nearly 2 years, before he gains insight into his situation. There is a clear lack of self-assertion to deal with his situation. He escapes (e.g., smoking, parking elsewhere) rather than trying to solve the problem.

Last but not least, there seem to be deficiencies in the personnel system. The fact that a boss like MC can survive in this organization and can stay there for years without intervention or sanctions is troubling, to say the least.

Dominic can react in three ways, each with its advantage and disadvantage: exit, voice, and resignation.

Exit

He can quit the organization or try to find another job within the organization. The advantage of this solution is that it can increase his self-esteem ("I don't want to be manipulated and humiliated by my boss any longer") and that he hopefully can find a job where he can find job motivation and satisfaction. The disadvantage is that he has to take some risks financially, which he probably cannot afford due to the high loan for his house.

Voice

He can react against the situation and try to change it. He might find colleagues who are in the same situation and are willing to oppose the boss. It is easier to deal with a situation when one is not alone. They could ask for a meeting with the boss; if the boss feels that a lot of people criticize his behavior, this might make him change. Dominic could also inform the higher management or the personnel department of MC's behavior. They might be in a position to enforce another behavior (through training, systems of performance appraisal, or bonus systems) or to remove him from his position. If a system of bottom up evaluations is introduced in the organization, the dysfunctional behavior of the boss may become very clear. The advantage of this solution is that there might be a change in the situation and also that other colleagues can reap the fruits of Dominic's actions. The disadvantage might be that the boss is supported by the organization, and Dominic's actions become a boomerang: He might become the scapegoat in the organization and the boss might take revenge.

Resignation

Dominic can resign himself to the situation, which means that he tries to live with it. He can look for pleasure outside work and consider his work only as a means of income. The advantage of this solution is possibly greater happiness and psychological health (no need to go to a psychotherapist anymore), as he has acknowledged and accepted the conditions of his employment. The disadvantage is a low degree of work motivation and job satisfaction.

It appears that Dominic is leaning toward the third solution, probably due to his character (a low degree of self-confidence) and financial circumstances (a wife who no longer works and a sizable loan for his house). I would prefer the second solution. Dominic should stand up to his boss and seek the support of his colleagues, upper management, and the personnel system in his effort to rid the organization of a dysfunctional manager.

Annie Hondeghem is a professor at the University of Leuven, Belgium.

Andrea Quarantillo

This is the saga of Dominic and the Dominator, an all too classic situation. On the surface the problem appears to be an overbearing boss who does not value his new employee or any of his other employees for that matter. But in truth the problem is not a manipulative boss whose style is management by fear and intimidation. The problem is really a newly promoted manager who allows himself to be co-opted by the position and the salary to the point where he loses the ability to make independent decisions about his career and his life.

Dominic makes a classic mistake in this case study. Before he has a firm footing in his new position, he begins to live his life in the style to which he *wants* to become accustomed. Before he has any idea if he will like his new position or be successful at it, he buys a new, expensive home and has his wife quit her job. Therefore, when he becomes disenchanted with the position, he feels trapped by bills and debts, unable to leave an untenable situation.

Early on in his tenure, Dominic realizes that his boss, MC, is a manipulator and that he intimidates staff. Dominic tells us that he must be slow because it took him 6 months to come to this realization. Actually it is probably a normal amount of time to reach such a conclusion—any less might be too precipitous.

After 6 months, when Dominic realizes his predicament, he does the right thing. He makes an appointment to meet MC and discuss his concerns. This is a wise and prudent step because there is always the possibility that a superior could take the criticism seriously and agree to make some changes. Even if a superior doesn't take a subordinate's concerns seriously, it shows good faith to make an attempt to work out any differences. In addition, it is possible after discussing concerns with a first-line supervisor for an employee like Dominic to go to a second-line supervisor for assistance if there is no progress toward resolution. Unfortunately, this case study does not include anything about a second-line supervisor, so Dominic apparently does not have such an option in this situation.

Unfortunately for Dominic, MC does not take the criticism constructively but rather reacts by finding fault with Dominic. MC deals with Dominic by not so subtlety threatening him. He talks about the incompetence of Dominic's colleagues and how he has plans for pressuring them to resign or transfer. He advises Dominic to ignore his colleagues and not become one of them. Obviously, this is MC's way of letting Dominic know that if he continues to raise issues and complain, he too could find himself being pressured to resign or transfer.

Dominic makes another mistake when he allows MC to arrange for his membership in private, prestigious clubs. This is always risky when you're a public sector employee because of ethical considerations. The case study does not tell us if membership dues were part of the equation, but even if no money were involved, there still can be a perception of impropriety attached to the club membership, not to mention a perception of indebtedness to your boss. As such, it is something that a public sector manager like Dominic should avoid.

Thus far Dominic has made some mistakes and has taken some positive actions. Were he not such a hostage to his salary, at this point Dominic could have begun to look for another position, even if it meant a demotion and less money. However, Dominic is not willing to take such action and MC is a master manipulator. He begins to take Dominic for an emotional roller coaster ride. He puts Dominic down at every turn and significantly undermines his self-esteem and self-confidence, to the point where it begins to take a toll on his physical health. Just as Dominic is reaching a low point on the roller coaster ride, MC brings him in for a meeting, tells him how valuable he is, gives him a sizeable raise and invites him and his wife to dinner. Up goes the roller coaster. MC knows that his success comes from keeping employees off balance, never knowing what to expect next.

Dominic takes heart from this renewed validation of his worth and feels that he is again on the right track. He slips back into the routine, working harder than ever, but soon is rejected by MC and told he will be replaced. With that, Dominic's physical and emotional health, as well as his family life, deteriorate further.

Through this entire time, however, Dominic remains unwilling to make a change because of financial concerns. The job is ruining his health, family life, and career. Yet through it all Dominic remains focused not on what he can do to improve his life but on whom he believes is responsible for his misery. He has ceded control of his life to MC in return for a good salary and yet he blames MC for his problems.

Dominic can and should take control of his life back from MC. Look for another job, be willing to take a demotion and a salary cut if necessary, assess whether or not he should sell his expensive home or consider his wife going back to work. These are Dominic's options to improve his situation.

It is clear that MC will never change, so staying in the job is not a viable option. There is no one to go to about workplace concerns except

MC, no second-line supervisor, thus there is no choice but to make plans to leave the job or continue to suffer at the hands of a manipulative boss like MC. It is important, however, to be aware that if Dominic doesn't take control of his life and leave this job, MC's treatment will not improve but will, in fact, deteriorate until either Dominic is unable to function for health reasons or MC fires him.

Only Dominic can control his fate, and his life will never improve until he makes the compromises in his personal life that allow him to leave the "Workplace of Doom."

Andrea Quarantillo is the regional director of Citizenship and Immigration Services for the U.S. Department of Homeland Security.

Index

Accountability, manager,
  17–19, 91–95
Adubato, Steve, 116–117
Annecke, Eve, 96–97
Apartheid, 27–32, 108–115
Aristigueta, Maria P., 91–92
Ataiants, Janna, 43–47

Bearfield, Domonic A., 163–164
Becking, Koen M., 133–134
Bednarek, Andrew, 93–94
Berry, RaJade, 48–51
Blagojevic, Bojana, 20–23
Blake, Richard, 54–56
Bogui, Frederic, 38–40
Bojin, Jacques, 102–103
Brinkerhoff, Derick, 108–110
Brinkerhoff, Jennifer, 108–110
Bruce, Willa, 67–70
Budget issues faced by managers,
  38–40, 91–95, 122–127

Caprio, Raphael J., 177–179
Chavda, Kamal, 57–59
Chun, Myung Jean, 64–66
Clapper, Valiant, 122–123
Cloete, Fanie, 104–105
Colleges and universities
  involvement in community
    surveys, 36–37

programs in public
  management, 53, 67
public relations, 24–26,
  36–37, 102–107
recent graduates, 38–40,
  48–51, 122–127
sexual harassment in, 49–51
Communities
affected by war, 20–23,
  96–101
economic assistance to, 20–23
impoverished, 27–32, 57–59,
  85–90, 108–115
marketing, 57–59
nongovernmental organizations
  (NGOs) operating in,
  20–23, 96–101
outreach programs, 13–16,
  85–90
redevelopment, 27–32, 57–59,
  85–90, 96–101, 108–115
Community Outreach
  Partnership
  Centers (COPCs), 13–16
Computer systems, library,
  41–42, 128–132
Confidentiality, information,
  3–5, 73–78
Crime, 6–12, 79–84
Cunningham, Robert 124–125

Database information
  formal requests for, 3–5
  library systems, 41–42
  reasonable costs in
    obtaining, 4–5
Decision making, employee
    involvement in, 41–42,
    128–132, 157–162
De Koninck, Jessica, 60–63
Displaced workers, 54–56
Downsizing, 64–66, 170–176
Dubnick, Mel, 73–74
DuBro, Nancy Soper, 83–84

Economic assistance projects,
    20–23, 96–101
Employees. *See also* Managers
  dealing with overaggressive
    managers, 67–70, 177–185
  displaced, 54–56, 150–156
  downsizing, 64–66, 170–176
  friendships with managers,
    64–66, 170–176
  involvement in decision
    making, 41–42,
    128–132, 157–162
  moving up in management,
    52–53, 144–149
  romances with managers,
    48–51, 139–143
Eom, Tae Hoe, 157–158
Ethical dilemmas
  related to information
    confidentiality, 3–5, 73–78
  university public relations,
    102–107

Failures of managers to meet
    organizational expectations,
    7–12, 79–84
Foster Pedley, Jon, 165–166

Gabrielian, Vache, 111–112
Gonzales, Ray, 159–160
Grants
  proposals, 13–16
  training, 54–56, 150–156

Hammond, Kathryn, 13–16
Haruna, Peter F., 135–136
Hayes, Harry J., 95
HIV/AIDS epidemic, 43–47,
    133–138
Hondeghem, Annie, 180–182
Hou, Yilin, 75–76
Humiliation, 67–70, 177–185

Information
  confidentiality, 3–5, 73–78
  database, 3–5, 41–42
  ethical dilemmas related to
    releasing, 3–5, 73–78
  implementing new computer
    resources for, 41–42,
    128–132
  reasonable costs of
    obtaining, 4–5
  time deadlines for providing
    and obtaining, 3–5
  volatile, 5
International Standards
    Organization (ISO), 54–55,
    150–156
Isaacs, Hedy, 150–152
Isolation, 61–62, 122–123

Joseph, Alma, 139–140
Josephson, Jyl, 137–138
Justice, Jonathan, 128–129

Kearney, Richard C., 79–80
Kenny, Gail, 130
King, Cheryl Simrell, 85–87

Laubsch, Paulette, 54–56
Lee, Seok-Hwan, 170–172
Libraries, 41–42, 128–132

Majumdar, Sarmistha Rina,
    131–132
Managers. *See also* Employees
    accountability of, 17–19,
        91–95
    advancement of, 52–53,
        144–149
    budget issues faced by, 38–40,
        91–95, 122–127
    and community-based
        programs, 13–16, 85–87
    contracts, 10–12, 79–84
    dealing with downsizing
        employees, 64–66,
        170–176
    defensive, 10–11
    failures to meet expectations,
        7–12, 79–84
    friendships between
        subordinates and, 64–66,
        170–176
    involving staff in decision
        making, 41–42, 128–132
    library, 41–42, 128–132
    loyalty of public servants to,
        3–5, 73–78
    manipulative, 67–70, 177–185
    morale, 52–53, 144–149
    municipal services, 17–19
    newspaper reporting
        on, 10–11, 33–37,
        81, 116–121
    overaggressive, 67–70,
        177–185
    performance reports, 17–19,
        91–95
    police, 7–12, 79–84

recruitment of, 8–10, 79–84
reorganization of, 41–42,
    60–63, 65–66, 128–132,
    163–169
results-oriented, 7–12
romances between subordinates
    and, 48–51, 139–143
sexual harassment charges
    against, 49–51, 139–143
Mandela, Nelson, 27
Manghisi, Rosanne, 81–82
Manipulative managers,
    67–70, 177–185
Marketing
    cities, 57–59
    colleges and universities, 24–26
Mathur, Navdeep, 167–169
McCourt, Willy, 153–154
Medicines to People, 43–47
Meyer, I. H., 118–119
Mo, Changhwan, 141
Morale, 52–53, 144–149
Morgan, Phil, 98–99
Morley, Susan, 106–107
Municipal services
    increased demand for limited,
        38–40, 91–95, 122–127
    isolated, 61–62, 122–123
    marketing, 57–59
    overemphasis on rank and
        status within, 57–59,
        67–70

National Association for the
    Advancement of Colored
    People (NAACP), 16
National Economic Development
    Agency (NEDA), 64–66
National Metropolitan
    Development
    Agency (MDA), 13–16

Nelson, Carl W., 173–175
Newman, Meredith, 142–143
Newspapers
  information provided to,
    3–5, 73–78
  reporting on community-based
    programs, 15, 16, 90
  reporting on managers,
    10–11, 33–37,
    81, 116–121
Nongovernmental organizations
  (NGOs)
  conflict resolution, 99–101
  funding, 43–44
  international, 20–23,
    96–101, 133–138
  involved in fighting HIV/AIDS,
    43–47, 133–138
  local development projects by,
    137–138
  maintaining the grantor/grantee
    relationship, 138
  operating after apartheid's end,
    27–32, 108–115
  training, 44–47

Office romances, 48–51,
  139–143
Orosz, Janet Foley, 144–146

Paddock, Susan C., 120–121
Palyvoda, Lyuba, 100–101
Parking tickets, 3–5
Paxton, Helen, 24–26
Performance reports, 17–19,
  91–95
Piotrowski, Suzanne J., 3–5
Police organizations, 6–12,
  79–84

Poverty and community
  redevelopment, 27–32,
  57–59, 85–90, 108–115
Public information act, 3–5,
  73–78
Public relations and
  communications
  college and university,
    24–26, 36–37, 102–107
  between managers and
    employees, 157–162
  between public managers
    and community members,
    27–32, 57–59, 85–87
  between public managers
    and newspapers, 33–37,
    81, 116–121

Quarantillo, Andrea, 183–185

Rank and status overemphasis,
  57–59, 67–70
Reasonable costs of obtaining
  information, 4–5
Recruitment of leaders,
  8–10, 79–84
Redevelopment, community,
  27–32, 57–59, 85–90,
  96–101
Reidy, Terence J., 33–37
Reorganization, management,
  41–42, 60–63, 65–66,
  128–132, 163–169

Sayed, Yusuf, 147–148
School bonds, 3–5, 73–78
Schout, Adriaan, 113–115
Schwartz, Ray, 41–42
Schwella, Erwin, 6–12

Sexual harassment,
    49–51, 139–143
Smit, Babette, 77–78
South Africa
    apartheid in, 27–32
    community redevelopment
        in, 27–32, 108–115
    crime in, 6–12, 79–84
Soviet Union, 43–47,
    133–138
Swilling, Mark, 27–32

Training
    for displaced workers,
        54–56, 150–156
    grants, 54–56, 150–156
    nongovernmental organization
        (NGO), 44–47

Unemployed workers, 54–56,
    150–156
United Nations, 43

Van der Molen, Karel, 17–19
Van der Wiel, Ton, 161–162
Van Wyk, Belinda, 17–19, 52–53

Widrich, Francine, 176
Williams, Ethel, 155–156
Wish, Naomi, 149
Workforce development
    programs, 54–56, 150–156
Wray, Lyle, 88

Yang, Kaifeng, 89–90

Zhamierashvili, Andi, 126–127

About the Editors

Kathe Callahan (PhD, Rutgers University) is an assistant professor of public administration at Rutgers, the State University of New Jersey, Campus at Newark. She publishes on the topics of citizen participation, social capital, and performance measurement. Her current research includes a study on the relationship between citizen participation and government performance. She has traveled extensively throughout Russia and Central Asia recruiting students for graduate studies in the United States. Along with Dorothy Olshfski, she is a founding member of the South African Public Administration and Management Association (SAPAM).

Dorothy Olshfski (PhD, Temple University) is an associate professor of public administration at Rutgers University–Newark Campus. She teaches courses in leadership, analytic decision-making techniques and research design. Her published research is on organizational commitment, empowerment, and executive behavior. She was managing editor of *Public Performance and Management Review* for 6 years and is the originator and editor of the case analysis section of that journal. She has taught at the University of Cape Town and has traveled extensively throughout South America and Southern Africa.

Erwin Schwella (PhD, Stellenbosch) is a professor of public leadership and the director of the School of Public Management and Planning of the University of Stellenbosch, South Africa. He is also a consultant and advisor to ministers and other executive office holders in all spheres of government in the democratic South Africa. He has authored more than 30 academic publications in the fields of governance, leadership, organization development, and public management. He serves and has served on the editorial boards of a number of national and international academic journals. He is a National Research Foundation rated researcher in South Africa and a member of the Board of Overseers of the Center for Public Leadership in The Hague, the Netherlands.